ARIZONA'S HAUNTED ROUTE 66

ARIZONA'S HAUNTED ROUTE 66

DEBE BRANNING

Haunted America

Published by Haunted America
A Division of The History Press
Charleston, SC
www.historypress.com

Cover image: Old Route 66 in western Arizona. *Courtesy of Chance Houston.*

First published 2021

Manufactured in the United States

ISBN 9781467146661

Library of Congress Control Number: 2021941051

Notice: The information in this book is true and complete to the best of our knowledge. It is offered without guarantee on the part of the author or The History Press. The author and The History Press disclaim all liability in connection with the use of this book.

This book is dedicated to all of my road trip buddies past, present and future who have always humored me in my quest to explore old highways, historic tourist spots, and visit with the "ghosts" that remain behind.

CONTENTS

CONTENTS

CONTENTS

ACKNOWLEDGEMENTS

I would like to give a shout-out to all of the knowledgeable paranormal investigative teams, tour guides, tour companies, historians and amazing location owners who willingly shared their information, experiences and tales of the unknown to fill these pages with the phenomena they have encountered. I also want to thank friends and team members who accompanied me on road trips in order to explore various Route 66 locations, participate in the interviews and photograph some of the spectacular views.

A special thanks goes out to the AZ Route 66 Road Trip Crew, who painstakingly traveled all 385 miles with me to help make this book possible! Thanks to those who have traveled the Mother Road with me in the past, and kudos to my photo and manuscript editors!

My wish is for other historians and paranormal investigators to take the time to hop in their vehicles and partake in an adventure along the Mother Road before its glamour is just a wispy ghost of the past. I often say, "History and mystery go hand in hand," so I'm hoping that these stories will carry on the legacy of Arizona's Route 66 for many years to come. Road trip!

INTRODUCTION

Many of us remember that almost monumental feeling of overwhelming excitement that first week of June—the day school let out for the summer! Mom and Dad scrimped and saved all year so they could afford to load up the kids in the back of the station wagon and (if you were fortunate) head out on the road for a one-week vacation visiting historic landmarks and national monuments and buying souvenirs at various trading posts. If you were like my family, a cooler was packed with a picnic lunch to cut down on the cost of the burger joints we passed as we drove slowly through towns and cities. We ate our lunch at roadside stops on weathered picnic tables under a tree. If we were lucky, there might be a barbecue pit and a trash barrel, and if it was really fancy, there might be a smelly outhouse (surrounded by flies) nearby.

Bathroom breaks were only acknowledged when Dad needed to stop for gasoline. Gas station attendants serviced the vehicle while Mom gathered the coveted key to the restroom (most often secured on a ring with a large wooden stick marked "Men" and "Women"). The restrooms were greasy and smelly, with spiderwebs in the corner. If you were lucky, there was a roll of toilet paper sitting on the sink. But never fear—Mom always had a spare roll in her purse.

After supper, our parents drove down the old highways searching the neon signs for that perfect motel to rest our heads. No fancy hotels or swimming pools for our family! It was down to the basics: a bed with clean sheets and a sterile bathroom. If we were lucky, there was a café adjacent to the motel where we might be treated to a warm hamburger or hot dog.

No matter what, we loved being on the old highways. I can remember having to stop and change a burned-out headlight or maybe fixing a flat tire or two, but it was always an adventure. You would see all sorts of other families out on the road creating their own memories.

Route 66 was probably the most sought-out highway for vacationing travelers in the 1940s, 1950s and 1960s. But in its earlier days, it was also a road for survival. In the early 1920s, automobiles became affordable to many American households. They were being mass-produced in factories, and people started buying them at an astounding rate. To meet the needs of the public, the U.S. government created a federal numbered highway system that linked existing roads together into routes for people to travel. The official birthdate of Route 66 was November 11, 1926.

Route 66 consisted of 2,448 miles of blacktop roadway in eight states—from Chicago, Illinois, to the ocean views of Santa Monica, California. In between, travelers explored Missouri, Kansas, Oklahoma, Texas, New Mexico and Arizona—places most travelers had never dreamed of seeing. The cities and towns offered museums, attractions,

Old Route 66 in western Arizona. *Courtesy of Chance Houston.*

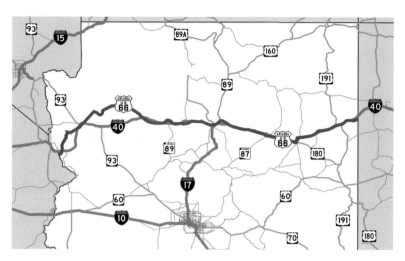

Arizone Route 66 map. *Courtesy of Pinterest.*

cafés with inviting home-cooked meals, cozy places to rest your head and plenty of trading posts to buy postcards and silly souvenirs. As time passed, traveling changed for motorists. Suddenly, travel was all about how quickly they could arrive at their destination. Interstate Highway 40 was planned and developed, and by 1984, most of the small towns and business had been bypassed, left to become ghost towns in the dusty Arizona desert.

Some say that Arizona has the most isolated stretches of Old Route 66 of all the states the road passes through. There is nothing like driving the dark, deserted highway in the middle of the night, listening to an oldies radio station as you navigate the narrow winding road. Stop at one of the remaining roadside tables and take in the sights—the view of the constellations and the Milky Way hovering over you will lead the way. Listen for the spirit voices of the past. They may be willing to share their tales, legends, folklore filled with hope and adventure, love and despair—it is all on Arizona's haunted Route 66.

CHAPTER 1

LUPTON

CHIEF YELLOWHORSE TRADING POST

Lupton is a tiny hamlet in Apache County adjacent to the Arizona/New Mexico state line along Route 66. This area of Arizona has been inhabited for at least ten thousand years. In more recent times, the Anasazis, or Ancestral Puebloans, lived in this area. Their homeland covered the Colorado Plateau, a vast part of southern Utah, Colorado, western New Mexico and Arizona west of the Colorado River and north of the Little Colorado and Puerco Rivers. Apache County was created in 1879, and in 1895, Navajo County was split from its western half. The Atlantic & Pacific Railroad, which later became a part of the Atchison, Topeka & Santa Fe (AT&SF), built its rails westward from Gallup and extended its tracks in 1883 following the Rio Puerco to the West River.

The town was named after the 1905 Winslow train master, G.W. Lupton. Another source indicates that G.W. Lupton owned the first trading post in the area. A small post office opened in 1917, and shortly after, in 1926, Route 66 was aligned through Lupton following the National Old Trails Highway, which had been created in the early 1910s. Lupton figured in the 1927 *Rand McNally Map*, along U.S. 66, as being twelve miles east of Houck, Arizona, on an unpaved but "graded road" that would be realigned once again in 1930.

Chief Yellowhorse Trading Post near Lupton. *Author's collection.*

Lupton is also known as "Painted Cliffs" for its soaring sandstone cliffs, formed between 60 and 200 million years ago. Statues of bear, deer and eagles adorn the top of the cliffs and welcome weary travelers to the deserts of Arizona. The 1940 Hollywood epic *The Grapes of Wrath* used the stop as a film location. Moviegoers may remember it as the spot where the Joad family enters Arizona beneath the colorful red cliffs. A state inspection booth once stood where Tom Joad reassures the inspector that they "don't intend to stay in the state any longer than it takes to cross it."

The Yellowhorse family has welcomed traveling tourists from their Navajo-owned trading post on the Navajo reservation for decades. They began their legacy as traders in the 1950s from a roadside stand, where the enterprising family sold Navajo rugs and petrified wood to vacationers. Traveling Route 66 was a great adventure, and stops were few and far between. Resources for gas, restrooms and food were greatly needed, so they created a traveler stop the entire family could enjoy.

Earlier in the 1940s, Harry "Indian" Miller left Two Guns, Arizona, and brought a portion of his famed desert zoo and Native American artifacts to the cave-like formation in Lupton. Here he proclaimed that he was an amateur archaeologist. Miller believed that he had discovered the "real" route to Coronado and the Seven Cities of Cibola in the Lupton area. Miller was quite the storyteller, and his accounts of the killings predating his arrival were rarely questioned. He opened a trading post in the "Cave of the Seven Devils," adorned with relics and wigwams to create an early Indian village. The name was painted in huge letters over the cave entrance and was visible from the highway. Some say that he resided at the cave until his death in February 1952, while others proclaim that Miller was banished from Arizona due to his unorthodox business practices. We will speak more of the infamous Harry "Indian" Miller in a future chapter.

In the 1960s, Juan and Frank Yellowhorse bought the site where Harry Miller's former "mystical" trading post stood and turned it into a modern trading center not far from their first primitive rug stand. The large cave still lends an aura of mystique and attracts Route 66 travelers as they enter the colorful deserts of Arizona.

Chief Yellowhorse Trading Post
Exit 359, I-40
Lupton, AZ 86508

CHAPTER 2
ALLENTOWN

CRONEMEYER TRADING POST

Allantown had its start around 1900 after the Atlantic & Pacific Railroad was extended to reach that point in 1881 and 1882. The community was named after Allan Johnson, a cattleman. The town post office was later renamed Allentown, changing the spelling, and established in 1924. It remained in operation until 1930. The town was long inhabited by the Navajo people of the area but never grew very large. When Route 66 came bustling through town, it boasted a gas station, grocery store, curio shop and café. For many years, travelers along this stretch of the road associated Allentown with a large dome-like structure that housed a curio shop called Indian City. Although the dome structure is gone, visitors can now visit a new modernized version of the famed site.

One of the first businessmen of the area was a man of German descent named Curt Cronemeyer. Some believed that he was a wealthy man and owned a large estate in Germany. Cronemeyer owned several trading establishments and erected a trading post a short distance south of the railroad tracks. Cronemeyer had two Navajo wives and built his trading business on land that was said to have been allotted to one of his wives by her family. He had two children: a son named Hoska Cronemeyer and a daughter named Edith Cronemeyer Murphy.

Cronemeyer had a reputation of being an eccentric character and somewhat of a flirtatious ladies' man. He often left a questionable impression

Cronemeyer Trading Post token. *Courtesy of Pinterest/eBay.*

on his traders and customers but was known to be an honest man and respected by those who knew him well. He was widely known throughout western New Mexico and eastern Arizona and had many friends among the Native American tribes.

On June 27, 1915, he and his employee, C.A. "Red" McDonald, were robbed, shot and killed at the trading post. At first, rumors began to circulate that the fifty-nine-year-old trader was confronted by Navajo tribesmen. However, newspaper articles later revealed that Gallup, New Mexico sheriff Bob Roberts tracked a group of Mexican bandits to El Paso, Texas, where they confessed to the murders when captured.

Victor Wezer and Blas Lozano, along with two other men, M. Nuanez and Delbino Rosales, secured five dollars in money from Cronemeyer and spent the entire amount for food. They rode out to their camp in the hills, where they cooked and ate what they had purchased.

Later, around six o'clock, they went back to the store, where they got into an argument with Red McDonald. Lozano whipped out his six-shooter, a .44-caliber, and shot McDonald dead, putting two bullets in his body. Lozano later stated that it was not their intention to kill either of the men in the store when they returned, but a quarrel came up over an old watch that they were trying to pawn for more money. After McDonald was shot by Lozano, Wezer pulled out his revolver, a .38-caliber, and opened fire on Cronemeyer.

As he stated it, they "had to kill Cronemeyer so he could not tell the story of the killing of McDonald." Six shots in all were fired, according to his testimony. Wezer shot Cronemeyer twice, he said, once through the hand and once through the body. A third shot was fired, but this bullet went wild and struck the wall of the store.

Cronemeyer was not instantly killed and was able to get to the telephone and call for help. At about 8:00 p.m., a telephone call was received at Houck, Arizona, and a voice believed to have been Cronemeyer cried into the receiver, "We are shot! Send help quick, quick, quick!" The Santa Fe Railroad pumper and section foreman went at once on horseback, and upon arrival at the trading store, they found McDonald dead behind the counter of the store and Cronemeyer lifeless on the bed. McDonald was shot through the eye and breast. Trading checks and a box of crackers lay on the

Grave of "Red" McDonald at Hillcrest Cemetery, Gallup, New Mexico. *Author's collection.*

counter, indicating that the murdered man had been waiting on a customer at the time of the shooting. A Winchester rifle with one empty shell, covered with blood, lay beside him.

Footprints and drops of blood show that Cronemeyer ran around the house two or three times, either chasing or being chased by someone. A bloody handprint on the mirror in the living room indicated that he stopped to look at his reflection in the mirror. There was another bloody handprint on the floor of the kitchen, where he either fell or stooped.

For days, there was absolutely no clue to the identities of the perpetrators of the double murder. Shortly after the crime, two Mexicans were arrested but were later released for lack of evidence. An Indian was arrested, but he was released as well. An overcoat labeled with the name Ned Nuanez and found in the house offered a clue. Cronemeyer was known to have had several enemies, and it is said that threats had been made against him in the past. The bodies were brought to Gallup, New Mexico, and buried at the cemetery.

For three days, the bandits hid out in the hills. Wezer became tired and hungry and rode to Gallup, where he stayed for a day and then headed to a lumber camp. Rosales soon followed, and the two men began to argue—each accusing the other of the murders. They rode a freight train from Albuquerque to El Paso, according to their confession. Blas Lozano was arrested in August by Deputy Sheriff Pipkin of McKinley County, who took his prisoner back to Gallup on Santa Fe train no. 1.

Sheriff Roberts of nearby Gallup was credited for tracking the group of Mexican bandits, who had ridden down to El Paso, Texas. The men eventually confessed to the murder and were apprehended. The four men implicated in the murders were refugees from Old Mexico, and it was the fear of being caught by Pancho Villa and hanged for treason that prevented them from crossing back into Mexico after the killing spree.

Curt Cronemeyer was buried at Hillcrest Cemetery in Gallup, New Mexico.

CHAPTER 3

HOUCK

FORT COURAGE

Houck was founded by James D. Houck (1848–1921), a mail carrier working a route from Prescott, Arizona, to Fort Wingate, New Mexico. In 1874, he established a trading post called Houck's Tank. The original structure was built using sandstone and held together with mud and mortar. He also ran a herd of sheep in the same area (a trade he learned from the nearby Navajos) in addition to operating the trading post. In 1880, William Walker and William Smith were murdered by Native Americans at the trading post. Violence seemed to follow James Houck wherever roamed, and his reputation grew more deadly through the years.

Houck left the post in 1885 and moved to the Mogollon Mountains, where he had large cattle and sheep interests. He served as a representative in the Arizona Territorial Legislature. Houck became an Apache County deputy sheriff under the notorious Commodore Perry Owens when the deadly Pleasant Valley War between sheepherders and cattlemen erupted in 1887. During the ongoing conflict, William Graham was shot and killed on August 17, 1887. Graham lived long enough to identify Ed Tewksbury as the assailant. But later, James D. Houck would publicly declare that it was he who fired the shot that killed the man. In the following years, he became involved in the lynching of three cattle rustlers. He soon felt that it was time to move his sheepherding operation to Cave Creek—just north of Phoenix.

Nicknamed the "Cave Creek King," Houck operated a shearing camp for the local sheep men. He established a boardinghouse and saloon for the herdsmen from the northern mountains during the winter months. The boardinghouse served as a community center, hosting many local events. The Houcks advertised their homestead as a health resort and rented houses along the stream to folks with tuberculosis.

James Houck committed suicide at his home in Cave Creek, Arizona, by taking a lethal dose of strychnine in 1921. Earlier, before committing the act, Houck told friends that he was tired of living. Houck went into the house after feeding his chickens and stated that he had taken the strychnine. He lay down on a bed and requested that his shoes be removed, as he did not care to die with them on. Efforts to counteract the poison failed. He was seventy-four years old and had been a part of Arizona history for more than forty-five years. He is buried at Greenwood Cemetery in Phoenix.

The old trading post in Houck went through several hands and was operated until 1922. About that time, the highway was moved farther north of the railroad. Unlike many of the other small towns located on Route 66, the passing traffic had little or no effect on the small town of Houck—that is, of course, until Interstate 40 turned Route 66 into a "ghost highway."

Vintage Fort Courage Trading Post postcard. *Courtesy of Route 66 Postcards.*

Fort Courage Trading Post in Houck. *Author's collection.*

Today, it is the site of a large modern ghost town—Fort Courage—a replica of the fort seen in the TV series *F Troop*. The series was not filmed here, but somehow it became a favorite tourist stop along Route 66 in the late 1960s and early 1970s. There was a restaurant, a post office and a convenience shop on the property. It also featured motel units, a trailer park and a campground. Guests flocked to climb the fort's tower, which mimicked the set of the popular TV show.

For some reason, the parking lot of the ill-fated tourist destination became the perfect scenario for crime and hostage negotiations along Route 66 and, later, I-40. In 1979, a woman traveling on a Greyhound bus discovered that her purse was missing $660 when she hopped off the bus to grab a bite to eat at the Fort Courage exit.

When a Gallup, New Mexico gas station was robbed in September 1980, the bandits abducted three station attendants in a stolen vehicle and later freed them in the parking lot at Fort Courage. The robbers were heavily armed with ammo and a sawed-off shotgun.

On a cross-country bus in October 1990, a Glendale, Arizona man, armed with a semiautomatic weapon, planned to hijack the bus with thirty-five passengers on board. Their smart-thinking bus driver pulled into the Fort Courage parking lot after alerting the law. With snipers in position, the hostages were able to evacuate the bus. The would-be disaster was diverted after three hours of negotiations. Do the emotions of these terrified victims still haunt this isolated piece of asphalt?

We visited the abandoned Fort Courage in October 2020. It was a cold, windy day, but one could almost hear the laughter of children frolicking up in the watchtower, donning wool and red felt cowboy hats laced in white ribbon while Dad filmed the moment with the old Bell and Howell movie camera. The energy of spirits is still part of the residual "reruns."

Fort Courage
I-40, Exit 348
Houck, AZ 86506

ABANDONED QUERINO CANYON BRIDGE

About four miles southwest of Houck is the Old Route 66 Querino Canyon Bridge, which spans the rugged Querino Canyon. The State of Arizona built the bridge in 1929 as part of the 1926–31 relocation alignment of Route 66 across Northern Arizona. You can't miss locating the example of highway truss design and its steel lattice guardrails—typical for the time of the two-lane roadway. This section of the highway became a bumpy country road during the 1960s after the completion of I-40. The historic Querino Canyon Bridge still carries traffic to the Navajo reservation.

Querino Canyon Bridge. *Courtesy of Wikimedia.*

The old bridge has had its share of deaths of highway travelers along Route 66. In August 1950, a family traveling from Gallup, New Mexico, crashed into the bridge, killing one of the passengers. A gentleman was thrown and crushed between the car and a cement abutment of the Querino Canyon Bridge. Stand there on a quiet night—do you hear the echoes from the canyon below?

The 269-foot Querino Canyon Bridge crosses Querino Canyon 3.8 miles southwest of Houck as part of Old Highway 66. Just across from the bridge, you should be able to spot the ghostly ruins of the old Querino Canyon Trading Post.

CHAPTER 4
SANDERS

THE LOG CABIN TRADING POST

The origin of the Sanders name has been a hot topic for many years. While some historians insist that the town was christened after a railroad office engineer, C.W. Sanders, other locals believe it received its moniker from Art Saunders, who operated a trading post in the area. The railway station was given the name Cheto to avoid confusion with another station called Sanders that had already been established along the line.

Confused already? The settlement of Cheto along the Atchison, Topeka & Santa Fe Railroad gained its first post office in 1896, but it lasted only a few years. The need for the post office seemed inconsistent with an on-and-off population growth of the town. In 1932, the name was changed back to Sanders. The town became an educational center for displaced Navajos; the Navajo-Hopi land dispute started in the 1860s and was in and out of the courtrooms for at least twenty-five years.

Trading posts were the main source for supplies for travelers, Native Americans and local residents. One of the first stores established was run by G.W. Sampson in 1883—the same building that Art Saunders would later operate. Trading posts would come and go, but one of the long-lasting posts that graced Route 66 was the Cedar Point Trading Post. It opened in 1928 and was owned and operated by a variety of proprietors until 1980. Most of the old trading posts are gone, but visitors can still stop at Burnham's

Vintage Log Cabin Trading Post postcard. *Courtesy of Route 66 Postcards.*

Trading Post. The current building is only about thirty years old, but the Burnham family has owned the trading post continually since the 1890s.

Another popular establishment was the Log Cabin Trading Post, operated by Al Berry for more than twenty-five years. It was built of pine logs and known for its illicit gambling rooms and government raids. There were slot machines and gambling tables where innocent travelers along Route 66 were fleeced of their bank rolls on a daily basis in a fast game of three-card Monte. Three slot machines were seized in 1947, and Berry was fined $1,500.

Berry advertised the location as the "Largest Free Zoo in the Southwest" and enticed tourists to see the "Donkey with the Live Human Head" and Native American ruins he excavated. Over the years, Berry filled his trading post with ancient mementos of the Old West: music players, guns and clothing out of the bloodthirsty past. He sold ornate Navajo-made jewelry and other items pawned by the Indians who traded at his store. There are still a few ruins and a wishing well on site west of the current Ortega Indian Ruins Store. It is the best place to start collecting juniper seed (ghost beads) bracelets. The jewelry is supposed to ward off bad spirits and nightmares and help protect you.

Sanders is located near I-40 and the BNSF Railway. Old Route 66 ran near the town, and a few sections of the Mother Road still exist here. Look for the old Sanders Bridge on an abandoned section of Claymine Road (former US 66). Built in 1923, the Pratt pony truss bridge over the Puerco River is listed in the National Register of Historic Places. It is closed to vehicle traffic, but pedestrians may still explore the bridge on foot.

Many travelers in the area claim that they have seen a hitchhiking ghost walking along Route 66 on the outskirts of town. Legend says that the spirit was run over and killed more than eighty years ago at the very spot he is seen on the roadway. His soul and energy may have never left the site. Drivers state that they have pulled over to offer the man a ride, but the specter disappears as they slow down. When cruising alongside the ghost, it stays in sight. But look in the rear-view mirror and the phantom hitchhiker has vanished. They claim that this is not an optical illusion and that he looks like a live person dressed in old-fashioned clothing. Another tragic ghostly victim of Old Route 66 was a spirited gambler left to wander the desert with no bus ticket. Then there's a spectral Native American in search of his family relics. Beware of offering a ride to just anyone wandering the roads.

CHAPTER 5

HOLBROOK

CURSE OF THE PETRIFIED FOREST

Only traces of the old roadbed and weathered telephone poles mark the original path of the famous Route 66 in the Petrified Forest National Park. It is the only park in the National Park System containing a section of the Mother Road between Chicago and Los Angeles.

Road trip travelers marvel over the small section of the Painted Desert of Arizona, where you can find forests of crumbled, forgotten trees preserved as stone. More than 200 million years ago, these large conifers were uprooted by floods, washed down through the highlands and later buried by the silt of the sandy floodplains. Water seeped through the barren wood and replaced decaying organic material cells with multicolored silica. The land was raised by geological upheaval, and soon erosion began to expose the long-buried petrified wood.

Early explorers of the region in the mid-1800s carried off pieces of wood as keepsakes. Wagons, trucks and early autos were filled to capacity with relics and hauled away to be sold as souvenirs.

When the Petrified Forest was named a National Monument in 1906, it became illegal to remove any specimens of petrified wood from the park. Theft of the wood can result in heavy fines. But that hasn't always stopped tourists and rock hounds from removing a piece of history from the park. Park officials report that twelve tons of petrified wood are stolen each year.

Old postcard of the Petrified Forest National Park. *Courtesy of Route 66 Postcards.*

Visitors think that no one would ever notice "just one little rock missing" or that anyone saw them toss that tiny wooden specimen in their backpack as they walked along the viewing trails. But they often learn later that it really wasn't the best plan after all.

In the 1930s, Route 66 visitors to the Petrified Forest began to report that after taking that one piece of petrified wood from the park, they were suddenly bombarded with bad luck. The curse continues today. There is even a room at the Rainbow Forest Museum at the Petrified Forest National Park dedicated to the hundreds of "cursed thieves" who hid just one small rock in their vehicle during their visit. Letters and e-mails of confession state that they encountered car problems during their travels, they lost their jobs, their house burned down or they developed medical conditions. Some became unemployed or even jailed! Envelopes and sometimes boxes of stolen rocks are received at the park on a regular basis.

The park has established what it calls the "Conscience Rock Pile," where it respectfully returns the stolen booty back to the Petrified Forest grounds. There is even a display in the museum called "Mystery of the Conscience Wood" where guests (who may be thinking the curse is a hoax) can sit on a bench and read a binder containing letters from all over the world from travelers begging forgiveness. The earliest "conscience letter" dates back to a traveler from 1935.

Petrified logs forever grace the national park. *Author's collection.*

One such letter stated, "Believe me....If I would have known the curse went with any of the rocks, I never would have taken these. My life has been totally destroyed since we have been back from vacation. Please take these so my life will get back to normal. Let me start over again. Forgive me for ever taking these rocks home."

Some of the letters include detailed maps asking the rangers to please return the artifacts to the exact place from where the petrified wood was stolen. The tourists are not the only believers in the superstitions and curse. In the past, traditional Navajos would not touch petrified wood because they also believed it to be cursed. In Navajo legends, pieces of the petrified wood, or *yei-bits-in*, were bones of the greatest and fiercest of all the alien gods—a strong and mighty giant named Yei tso.

But never fear! Tourists can purchase petrified wood collected legally from private land at a number of nearby businesses. These relics range in prices and are generally inexpensive, and of course, the curse does not come attached to them—fingers crossed.

Drive east from Holbrook about eighteen miles on US Highway 180 and then turn north onto Petrified Forest Road. You can also get to the park and visitors' center directly from I-40, Exit 311. Several gift shops are at the southern Highway 180 entry. 928-524-6228.

PAINTED DESERT INN

The Painted Desert Inn was built of petrified wood and other native stone under the direction of Herbert David Lore. Lore operated the "Stone Tree House" as a tourist attraction along Route 66. Visitors could stop for meals in the dining room, purchase Native American arts and crafts from local artists and sip on a cool drink in a downstairs taproom. Six small rooms with private entrances were available to travelers for two to four dollars per night. Lore offered two-hour tours of the Painted Desert and Petrified Forest below the inn.

A small oasis in the vast Painted Desert, the Stone Tree House was very isolated. The inn was not connected to electrical lines. A shop containing a lighting plant supplied electricity. Water was hauled in from the Puerco River. Lore wanted sell the property but also wanted the site to be preserved and protected for years to come. In 1931, the Petrified Forest National Monument purchased the Stone Tree House and a large section of nearby land.

After a few structural problems were detected at the inn, the building was restructured in a more southwestern style. Architect Lyle Bennett was successful in creating a new look for Painted Desert Inn. His team of Civilian Conservation Corps (CCC) workers used Ponderosa pine and aspen poles cut from Arizona forests for roofing beams and crossbeams. Light fixtures were hand-made from punched tin. Wooden tables and chairs were carved in Native American designs. There are beautiful skylight panels hand-painted by two of the CCC workers based on prehistoric designs from various archaeological sites in the Southwest. Even the floors were painted with patterns influenced by Navajo blanket designs. Once again, the Painted Desert Inn was graced with a new life. It attracted Route 66 travelers with meals, souvenirs and lodging.

With the onset of World War II, the CCC was disbanded as young men were sent off to war. Travel was suddenly halted by gas rationing. Sadly, the inn closed temporarily in October 1942. It was later rescued by the famous Fred Harvey Company. The company architect and interior designer, Mary Elizabeth Jane Colter, arrived in December 1947 and went to work creating a new color scheme; she placed windows in strategic walls of the inn so guests could soak in the magnificent views of the Painted Desert. Renowned Hopi artist Fred Kabotie was commissioned to paint beautiful murals in the dining room and lunch room walls, offering scenes of Hopi culture.

Painted Desert Inn. *Courtesy of Carolee Jackson.*

Wear and tear on the inn led to another closure in 1963, and its future was once again uncertain. With cracks and water damage, some folks believed that it was time for the building to be torn down. The park scheduled demolition of the building for 1975. However, the concerned public rallied a campaign to save the Painted Desert Inn, and it was listed as a National Historic Landmark in 1987. After years of preservation, the building became a museum and information center in 2006.

In the month of October, the center offers a "ghost tour" of the facility, with Petrified Forest park rangers offering tales of mystery and the potential reasons why the facility might be haunted.

Petrified Forest National Park ranger Rita Garcia told the story of a tragic fire inside the Painted Desert Inn on April 9, 1953. A park ranger arrived on the scene and broke down the locked door. Crawling on his hands and knees, he made his way through the smoked-filled building to find fifty-nine-year-old Marion Mace, the hotel manager, lying unconscious in her bedroom. The ranger carried the woman outside and set her down on the lawn. He bravely went back inside to save the historic structure by putting the flames out with a fire extinguisher. Unfortunately, the outcome for Mrs. Mace was not good. She died from smoke inhalation. No one knows what actually caused the fire, but most people suggested that the smoldering blaze was ignited by a cigarette. The flames started in the manager's bedroom, and it was noted that Mrs. Mace was rarely seen without a cigarette in her hand.

Ranger Garcia worked as a guide at the Petrified Forest for many years. It did not bother her that the old structure might be haunted. She once was quoted as saying, "Old buildings talk. They shift. They creak. You hear things."

The National Parks Traveler website mentions a few of the ghost stories that Ranger Garcia experienced:

> *The ranger was working on the main level one afternoon when she heard someone coming up the stairs from the tap room below. "It was footsteps on stone," she says, "but when I looked up to wave at the person coming up the stairs, no one was there."*
>
> *Other employees report hearing whispered conversations coming from unoccupied rooms, and some have wondered if Mrs. Marion Mace is still lingering around after closing time.*
>
> *After locking up one evening, one park ranger looked back through the windows and saw someone inside the museum walking from one room to another. Slightly irritated at the wayward tourist, the ranger unlocked the door and stepped inside. As soon as she entered the doorway, the ranger detected the unmistakable odor of cigarette smoke. Now the ranger was royally peeved. Not only was this tourist in a closed government building; the person had the gall to smoke in a museum! The ranger rushed from room to room in hot pursuit of her cigarette-smoking miscreant, until she realized there was no one in the building but her.*

The phantom smoker lingering inside the Painted Desert Inn is not the only unexplained phenomenon at the national park. There is also a mysterious spiral etched into a large boulder behind the ruins of Puerco Pueblo. Every summer solstice, as the sun rises, a shaft of light moves across the top and down the side of the large boulder. The beam of light hits the center of the small spiral at precisely 9:00 a.m. The significance of this ancient solar calendar remains unclear.

Painted Desert Inn
1 Park Road
Petrified Forest National Park, AZ 86028

HISTORIC NAVAJO COUNTY COURTHOUSE

Holbrook, located in the northeast part of the state, was founded in 1881. The quiet little town along Route 66 has not always been so serene. History shows that the seat for Navajo County was once as violent as its southeastern Arizona counterpart, Tombstone, and boasted of an equally deadly shootout in its streets.

Navajo County was known for its railroad, lumber, farm and ranch businesses, as well as for trade with the Native Americans. It attracted cowboys and criminals chased out of Texas and other nearby territories. Holbrook became a typical Wild West town filled with brothels, saloons and gambling houses. It was once said that Holbrook was "too tough for women and churches."

In 1898, Navajo County erected a new courthouse that would be the site of several notorious trials through the years. The basement of the courthouse housed the sheriff's office and jail cells. The cells were built in St. Louis, Missouri, and shipped to Holbrook via railroad flatcars. These small, dark cells were in continuous use for the next seventy-eight years.

Within a year of the opening of the beautiful Richardsonian Romanesque–style courthouse, it played host to one of the most controversial hangings of its day. The new courthouse jail was holding a murderer within its cells named George Smiley. He was convicted of killing a railroad section foreman and sentenced to hang on December 8, 1899. Arizona law required that the county sheriff send "invitations" of executions to the other Arizona sheriffs and territorial officials. Sheriff Frank Wattron issued a slightly sarcastic invitation, professionally printed on gilt-bordered paper. The weird invitation eventually ended up in the hands of President McKinley, who wired the Arizona governor. Smiley received a reprieve of thirty days from his execution, and a reprimand was issued to Wattron.

George Smiley was finally hanged on the courthouse grounds on January 8, 1900. He was the first and only man ever hanged in Navajo County. Some employees and visitors to the Navajo Country courthouse say that Smiley's spirit is still "hanging" around and has been seen wandering about the old courthouse and pacing up and down the staircase. The historical society staff blames the spirit for the opening and closing of doors, heavy footsteps on the second floor and strange voices and noises heard throughout the building. They even report that objects have mysteriously moved or disappeared.

Navajo Country Courthouse, built in 1899. *Courtesy of Carolee Jackson.*

The other resident ghost is said to have been a woman named "Mary." They say that Mary hanged herself in one of the jail cells. A former tourism director and his family were cruising past the courthouse one evening and noticed that some lights were left on in the building. He parked the car and went inside to turn them off. While he was inside the courthouse, his wife noticed a woman looking out of one of the windows. She ran inside to alert her husband, and together they searched the entire courthouse. Strangely, they did not find a living soul inside. A mysterious woman standing and peering out of an upstairs courthouse window has been seen by many visitors to the courthouse. Is it Mary still longing for freedom?

Cindy Lee and Debe Branning visited the Navajo County Courthouse to learn more about the ghosts and perhaps have their own encounter with one of the lingering spirits. The tour guide at the desk was very informative about the building's history and had a few ghost stories of his own. He mentioned that a team of paranormal investigators visited the facility in December 2008. Three psychics with the group felt the presence of several spirits in the building. Besides George Smiley and Mary, they sensed that the ghost of Sheriff Frank Wattron is still at his post, along with another gentleman and four children.

Above: Fringed purse at the Navajo County Courthouse. *Author's collection.*

Opposite: Prisoner cell at the Navajo County Courthouse. *Author's collection.*

The psychics announced that they were able to channel Mary in an upstairs room, so that was the first place Cindy and Debe visited.

Upstairs they found a bed, dresser bureaus and a few chairs in a tiny room. They placed an EMF meter on the bed and began to video the area. Debe sat her leather purse down on a chair and pulled out an audio recorder. They began to ask a series of questions. Out of the corner of one eye, Debe thought that she saw the fringe on her purse move. They both heard what sounded like faint footsteps enter the room. The ladies stood silent and waited to see what would happen next. Suddenly, they both saw the fringe on the purse flip into the air as if someone were running their fingers through it. Perhaps Mary was enjoying the feel of the fringe on what she thought was a leather buckskin bag.

Down in the jail cells, the guide was not sure why Sheriff Frank Wattron would be haunting the building. Debe explained that sometimes the dead come back to visit the places that were special to them. He may still believe that he is a protector of law and order within the courthouse. Debe noted

that Wattron and Smiley probably don't even "see" each other during their ghostly visits to the building.

Most recently, the Route 66 crew was escorted by the current guide to see a set of hidden cells not usually open to the public. Being the only visitors, they had full access to entire building and felt in awe at the Native American display where other guests had left offerings for better life and fortune.

Today, the historic building is home to the Holbrook Chamber of Commerce, a visitors' center and the Navajo County Historical Museum. It is a good location for investigators to begin their visit to Holbrook's haunted and historical places. They have a historical self-guided tour booklet that takes you to sites of gunfights and old saloons. You will soon learn that Holbrook was a big piece of Arizona's history and still is a favorite stop for spirits along Old Route 66.

Navajo County Historic Courthouse
Holbrook Chamber of Commerce
100 East Arizona Street
Holbrook, AZ 86045

BUCKET OF BLOOD SALOON

Near the old Santa Fe Railroad Depot was a dirt road handily lined with restaurants, bakeries and a Chinese laundry. There were drugstores, a mercantile and even a trading post. Along with these businesses came saloons, gambling halls and soiled doves.

Terrill's Cottage Saloon was just another drinking establishment in Holbrook until a bloody event changed its reputation and placed it on the list of notorious gun battle sites of the West. As a result of a simple poker game that ended in a drunken brawl and murder, the saloon will be forever known as the "Bucket of Blood."

Legend states that in 1896, Grat Dalton, who was a member of the notorious Dalton Gang, and another outlaw named George Bell were playing poker with two other men at the Cottage. A heated argument over a deal of the cards ended with Dalton firing shots from a .45 and killing the two men. The murdered card players fell side by side on the wooden saloon floor. Dalton and Bell quickly fled the Cottage and rode out of Holbrook. After the smoke settled, the bodies of the poker players were removed. The talk about town was that the floor where the dead men landed looked like a bucket of blood had been spilled, hence the new moniker.

Dalton was not arrested for the shooting; however, about six years later, back in Coffeyville, Kansas, his luck ran out. He was shot and killed with three other members of the Dalton Gang after a botched bank robbery attempt.

Side view of the Bucket of Blood Saloon. *Courtesy of Carolee Jackson.*

A different version of the story found in the *Coconino Sun* stated that on Sunday, January 19, 1896, a pistol shot was heard near the saloon. Two men were playing cards when suddenly a dispute arose and angry words passed between them. One man drew a revolver and forced the other to retreat to the street. In front of the drugstore, the aggressor fired, and his victim fell dead on the highway. The townsfolk rushed over to find his shirtfront crimson from the blood that flowed—he had been shot through the heart. The dead man was George C. Hiatt, a barber, and his slayer, Harry Donnelly, was the manager of the saloon. Hiatt's last words were, "Oh my God, he has shot me through the heart." He walked a few steps and then fell dead.

By the 1920s, the early Route 66 travelers found the Bucket of Blood Saloon to be a more respectable establishment. It stood next to a general store and across the road from a small gas station. The saloon drew in cross-country motorists, who stopped by to see the bullet holes in the walls and the famous stain on the dusty floor.

Today, the Bucket of Blood Saloon sits empty and long boarded up, closed for business. You can still get a look at the old drinking icon from the outside

Bucket of Blood painting at the Navajo County Courthouse. *Courtesy of Carolee Jackson.*

on Bucket of Blood Street. A historic self-guided tour of Holbrook points out the former businesses and structures on this once thriving thoroughfare. Residents claim that there were more than twenty-six shootouts on the street in front of the Bucket of Blood Saloon.

Mike Pool, a member of Southern Arizona Scientific Paranormal Investigators (SASPI), reported that the team picked up an EVP while sitting out in front of the building. Sounding like an old cowboy, the man used foul language and told them to "leave."

A painting that once hung in the Bucket of Blood Saloon is displayed at the Historic Navajo Country Courthouse Museum. Two bullet holes grazed the canvas during a drunken target practice in the barroom, as two patrons competed to see who could come closest to shooting the elk in the mountain lake scene. Hopefully the men were better shots while hunting game on a trail drive.

Travel south through old downtown Holbrook on Navajo Boulevard. Cross the railroad tracks to Bucket of Blood Street.

BLEVINS HOUSE

It was quite by accident that Debe Branning learned about the shootout in Holbrook, Arizona, at the Blevins House. This little-known incident ranks right up there with the gunfight at the OK Corral in Tombstone. Cindy Lee and Branning happened to be visiting the haunted Historic Navajo County Courthouse when the museum director told them the tale of Commodore Perry Owens and the notorious Blevins brothers. He drew the directions to the Blevins House on their map, and they dashed off to view the potential haunted site.

Commodore Perry Owens was born in Tennessee in 1852. He ventured from home at an early age and lived the life of a cowboy, working ranches in Texas and Oklahoma. Owens stood five-foot-ten, was rather slender and had intense light-blue eyes. He wore his long shoulder-length hair in the style of the mountain men and buffalo hunters. Owens was a man of few words and spoke with a southern drawl. By 1886, he had been elected sheriff of Apache County and immediately campaigned to "lay down the law."

Meanwhile, Andy Cooper (aka Andy Cooper Blevins) arrived to the Arizona Territory from Texas. He was the eldest son of Martin Blevins. Cooper was merely twenty-three years old and already had several run-ins with the law. He was somewhat of a bully, and he thrived on having power over the local ranchers and sheepherders. Crime and murder were second nature to him.

At Andy Cooper's urging, Martin Blevins headed to Arizona from Texas with the rest of his unruly sons: Charley, Hampton, John and Sam. The Blevins boys became partners with the Grahams of Pleasant Valley in eastern Arizona. An attack on the rival Tewksbury family resulted in the death of Hamp Blevins. The skirmishes in the war in Pleasant Valley were constant. Assaults on members of both families, Tewksbury and Graham, intensified, with Andy Cooper being in on many of the shootings. There was a three-day murderous standoff between the two families in 1887. Andy Cooper boasted that he was the murderer of one of the Tewksburys during those days. Commodore Perry Owens was ordered to arrest Andy Cooper.

On September 4, 1887, Owens rode into town and met with Sheriff Frank Wattron at the stables just down the road from the Blevinses' modest cottage. John Blevins caught wind of the meeting and dashed home to warn his half brother Andy.

Commodore Perry Owens, deciding to take on the Blevins brothers alone, grabbed his Winchester rifle and walked slowly toward their house. The

Site of the shootout at the Blevins House. *Author's collection.*

townsfolk of Holbrook gathered in the distance to witness what was about to unfold. Owens noticed that a man was watching him from an open door at the Blevins house. As he drew nearer, the door slammed shut.

Having been warned, Andy was busy saddling up his horse. He looked up to see Owens approaching the house and scurried inside to safety. There were two other men hiding inside the house—John Blevins and Mote Roberts—along with fifteen-year-old Sam Houston Blevins. Also home that day were Sam's mother, Mary Blevins; nine-year-old Artemisia; John's wife, Eva; their infant son; Amanda Gladden; her baby; and her nine-year-old daughter.

Owens stepped up to the porch and looked in the windows. He could easily see Andy, John and the others in the room. He called Andy out. The Blevinses took out their pistols. Andy raised his gun, but Owens fired his shot first, wounding Andy in the stomach. John Blevins jerked the door open and fired at Owens. The bullet missed, striking the getaway horse tied to the tree. Owens whirled around and fired a shot through the door, sending John to the floor. Owens then dashed back out to the street to take cover behind a wagon and to keep a steady eye on all parts of the house.

Owens noticed some movement near the front window. Andy Cooper had moved to the window and was preparing to take another shot at Owens. Owens fired his third shot, which tore through the wall of the house and entered Andy's hip. Young Sam Blevins grabbed Andy's gun and furiously ran out the front door to open fire on Owens. Commodore Perry Owens shot and took the lad down on the porch. Mote Roberts leaped out of the window with a six-shooter in hand ready to fire. Owen's fifth shot hit Roberts in the chest and dropped him in his tracks. After the smoke from the blazing guns settled, Samuel Blevins, Andy Cooper and Mote Roberts were dead. John Blevins survived his wounds. In a mere sixty seconds, only John Blevins was able to fire a shot, but it failed to find its mark. Owens fired five times at moving targets and did not miss a one.

The house where this bloodbath took place still stands near the corner of Joy Nevin Avenue and Second Street in Holbrook. It is now used as an extended care facility, but you are allowed to photograph the historic home from the street.

Southern Arizona Scientific Paranormal Investigators' Mike Pool reported that their team did an investigation on the property of the Blevins

Grave markers of those killed at the Blevins House. *Author's collection.*

House in 2016. They were hoping to record some EVPs from the spirits of the Blevins family, but they did not. They did, however, capture the sound of footsteps running away from the Blevins House on camera audio. Their team medium reported that the spirit of Samuel Blevins came through to say that Owens didn't give Andy Cooper a chance to draw and just shot him in the doorway of the Blevins house. Before the team left, they picked up an EVP that said, "Sam says thank ye."

Commodore Perry Owens later served as a U.S. marshal and settled in Seligman, Arizona. He died on May 10, 1919, and is buried at Citizens Cemetery in Flagstaff, Arizona. Blevins, Cooper and Roberts were buried side by side, just as they fought, at the Holbrook Cemetery.

Blevins House
Joy Nevin Avenue and Second Street
Holbrook, AZ 86025

WIGWAM VILLAGE MOTEL

The unique Wigwam Village Motel in Holbrook provides Route 66 enthusiasts the opportunity to "sleep in a Wigwam" just like our families did in the height of Route 66 travel in the 1950s, '60s and '70s. The Arizona motel owner, Chester E. Lewis, built the Wigwam Village in 1950. It's in a location full of Old West history and carries stories of many superstitions. There are fifteen wigwams, but they are numbered through sixteen because, per tradition, the number thirteen is skipped.

Does the ghost of Elvis stay at the Wigwam Village Motel? Debe Branning was conducting her annual road trip "Cemetery Crawl" event (a somewhat mild version of TV's *The Amazing Race*; instead of traveling to foreign countries and mysterious destinations, these folks travel across Arizona to historic attractions and cemeteries with interesting tales). While checking the teams into the famed Wigwam Village Motel, a man who happened to look just like Elvis pulled up and strolled into the lobby to claim a room of his own.

With his Elvis persona intact, the man posed for photos and retreated to his room in the circle of wigwams, with his vehicle out front with a personal license plate ("ELVIS," of course). The group joked how every year on the Cemetery Crawl they run into Elvis in some shape or form, whether it

Vintage Wigwam Motel postcard. *Courtesy of Route 66 Postcards.*

Debe meets "Elvis" at the Wigwam Motel. *Author's collection.*

be a statue, restaurant name, a room named for him or some other kitsch gimmick. The group went out to dinner at a local Route 66 diner and came back at about 9:00 p.m., prepared for a good night's sleep—after all, day two of the Cemetery Crawl would be upon them bright and early in the morning. At about 9:45 p.m., the neon lights in the motel parking lot turned bright. The sound of Native American drumming filled the air. Debe immediately thought that this must be some sort of "lights out" tradition the motel did each evening before bedtime. The drums pounded louder and louder. Curious, she slowly opened the door of her wigwam. There in the middle of the parking lot stood Elvis, holding a bright lantern and a boom box over his head.

"Just thought I'd have a little fun!" he said with that famous Elvis drawl. "Goodnight, hon!" Debe shut the door and began to giggle.

"Who was that?" asked Kenton Moore while watching the evening news on TV.

"Why, the ghost of Elvis of course!" She gave him a thumbs up.

The teams were up early the next morning. They enjoyed a quick breakfast before continuing the Cemetery Crawl and then headed back toward Phoenix. There was no sign of Elvis or the vehicle whose license plate bore his name. Does Elvis relive the best days of his life traveling up and down Old Route 66?

Gonna travel, gonna travel wild and free. I'm gonna pack my bags because this great big world is calling me.

—Elvis Presley

Wigwam Village Motel
811 West Hopi Drive
Holbrook, AZ 86025

CHAPTER **6**

JOSEPH CITY

ELLA'S FRONTIER TRADING POST

Joseph City was settled in 1876 by colonists from the Church of Jesus Christ of Latter-day Saints. This band of seventy-three pioneers was led by Captain William C. Allen, and they traveled to the Little Colorado River Basin of Arizona. Joseph City was one of four Little Colorado River colonies. The other colonies were Brigham City, Sunset and Obed. Joseph City is the only remaining colony.

The name of the colony changed twice after its establishment. The area settled by Captain Allen's group was called Allen's Camp in honor of their leader. There was a name change in January 1878 to St. Joseph. This change was brought about when the Little Colorado Stake was organized; it was suggested in order to honor founder Joseph Smith. In 1923, there was a final name change to Joseph City. Due to mail and freight shipment confusions, the Santa Fe Railway, which also ran through St. Joseph, Missouri, asked that St. Joseph, Arizona, change its name. The residents of the town voted, and the name became Joseph City.

The Frontier Trading Post was the last business owned by Frederick "San Diego" Rawson, born in Perry, New York, in December 1858. When he was about five years old, he headed west with a foster family out of Michigan. All was pleasant until the wagon train was attacked by the Cheyenne tribe. Rawson and his twin brother, Frank, were enslaved by the

Cheyennes until they were sold to the Arapahos for five horses. After two years, a U.S. Army regiment was able to rescue the pair of lads and send them back to Michigan. It would be another ten years before Rawson was ready to head back to the western frontier again. Frederick Rawson led a successful frontier life, with careers as a prospector, trapper and cowboy; he also shot bison and grizzly bears. He worked as a circus animal trainer and clown, found gold mines and published poems. People said that he resembled Mark Twain, and perhaps his tales of adventures were just that—we may never know! He eventually landed in Joseph City shortly after the commissioning of Route 66 and began to operate a museum in town. The museum displayed his personal collection of early western life with family household items such as furniture and tools. Sadly, business was not prosperous, and he sold his assortment of artifacts. Rawson moved to a small log building at the west end of town and opened his new venture, called Frontier Days Trading Post.

Later, he built an even larger log cabin building using discarded telephone poles, operating San Diego's Old Frontier, where he offered space on the property for local Navajo Indians to make and sell their jewelry, blankets and quilts. After twenty years in the trading post business, Rawson sold the Frontier Trading Post in 1947 to Ramon Hubbell, son of the famous Indian trader Don Lorenzo Hubbell. Frederick Rawson lived out his later years in Prescott, Arizona. He died in November 1951 at the age of ninety-two and is buried at the Arizona Pioneers Home Cemetery in Prescott.

The remains of Ella's Frontier Trading Post still stand along an abandoned section of Route 66 just outside the western boundaries of Joseph City. The once thriving business was owned and managed by Ella Blackwell, who purchased the property in 1955 after divorcing her second husband. Blackwell was a former student at the Juilliard School in New York City and kept a piano in the store. Occasionally, she entertained her customers with an impromptu recital. Ella Blackwell claimed that the trading post (formerly known as the Last Frontier Trading Post) was established in 1873, making it the oldest such establishment along Route 66. Ella, however, was often considered quite eccentric among friends and locals, so many patrons doubted her claim. Ella's Frontier Trading Post was always a classic tourist destination with vacationers. It is said that in her later years, Ella suffered from delusions and was often seen having conversions with imaginary people and animals—or were they merely the ghostly spirits of the past?

Ray Meany, who also owned the Hopi House Indian Trading Post west of Winslow, originally bought the Last Frontier, only to hand it over to his wife, Ella, who received the property as part of their divorce settlement. It was known as Ella's Frontier until her death in 1984. Other owners used the structure for various businesses, but sadly, it has been left to abandoned ruins along the south side of Old Route 66 for several years now.

CHAPTER 7

WINSLOW

LEORENA SHIPLEY: GHOST OF THE COTTONWOOD WASH

The lovely actress Leorena Shipley of Winslow, Arizona, met her death on Saturday, September 11, 1926, when a car in which she was riding caved in the western approach to the state highway bridge over the Cottonwood Wash, six miles east of Winslow.

Leorena was born in Iowa on September 28, 1897, the second daughter of Leo and Della Shipley. Her musical talents blossomed at an early age, when she started playing violin in kindergarten, and she soon mastered the clarinet as a child. The Shipley family moved west and made their home in Winslow, Arizona, where Leorena became active in sports and school plays. She graduated from Winslow High School in 1916 and won a scholarship to the University of Arizona in Tucson, where she studied theater and the arts. After graduating with a teaching certificate, she briefly taught school for two years back in Winslow.

After World War I, Leorena decided to fulfill her dreams of stardom and headed to California and the Oatman Theatrical School, where she adopted the stage name of "Norma Dean." Her performances were highly rated, and she became a popular stage star with fabulous reviews. She traveled to Salt Lake City and performed in the production *Three Live Ghosts*. Her parents were bursting with pride, and her father was quoted as saying, "We are mighty proud of you, may your star never dim, cling to your success by being a good girl."

Leorena Shipley photo, displayed at the Old Trails Museum in Winslow. *Author's collection.*

Sadly, her road to stardom would grow hazy just three years later. Leorena was back in Winslow to visit her family and friends. She decided to explore the Petrified Forest east of Holbrook with her mother and two acquaintances. The late monsoon rains poured down heavily that afternoon, filling the washes and riverbeds. Driving slowly in the storm at about 10:00 p.m., heading toward Winslow, the Shipley vehicle met up with an auto belonging to Vance Wilson, another family friend. Inside the vehicle was Wilson and Shipley's father, who had become concerned about the safety of the travelers due to the harsh weather conditions. Fearing that Manila Wash near Winslow was flooded from the heavy rain that afternoon, they set out to meet the Shipley party and assist them across the running washes.

Crossing the first wash offered no problems, and both vehicles easily traversed the rising waters. The two cars slowly headed for Cottonwood Wash, with the Wilson car leading the way about fifty feet ahead. The first car made it across without any difficulties, unaware of impending danger. Looking back, Mr. Shipley watched as the car behind him fell backward, its headlights going skyward into fast-swirling water and quicksand as the approach to the bridge collapsed.

Jumping out of the car before it came to a stop, Mr. Shipley ran back to the scene, where he found the auto lying on its side. The entire car was submerged except for the front corner of the driver's side. The window on the door was open. Tug Wilson, the driver, had managed to escape and was dragged to the road. Shipley and Tug then pulled Mrs. Shipley and Mrs. Ingledew from the vehicle, passing them up to Vance Wilson, who had turned his car around to aid the rescue effort. Tug shouted that Leorena was still missing and trapped inside the car.

Frantically searching the vehicle surrounded by moving water, Vance Wilson was lowered on a rope into the muddy rainwater and found the body inside the front of the car. He tried desperately to free her but failed. It was believed that she had been knocked unconscious by the impact of the accident, and her arm was tangled up in the steering wheel.

The other two women were taken at once to receive medical treatment in Winslow. Tug remained at the scene in the damp, cold, dark night, waiting for more volunteers to aid in the rescue. Scores of volunteer rescuers assisted in the effort of pulling the auto out of fifteen feet of quicksand. It took two days and two nights to retrieve the vehicle and the body. Grown men wept as Leorena's body was wrapped in blankets and transported back to town.

The citizens of Winslow were deeply saddened by this tragedy. Thousands of flowers, shipped in by train, covered her casket—most of them being the American Beauty Rose, a favorite of the actress. The final paragraph in her newspaper obituary read, "A great soul of light was gathered into the Soul of the Supreme Light, shining on forever." Leorena Shipley was buried at Winslow's Desert View Cemetery.

La Posada Hotel

La Posada Hotel, the last great railroad hotel, is a unique experience for travelers on Route 66. Built in 1930 for the Santa Fe Railway, La Posada is truly one of America's treasures. It was added to the National Register of Historic Places in 1992. The north side of the building faces Route 66 and was originally the back door. La Posada was designed for railroad passengers, so the front door faced the tracks on the south.

Mary Colter, the designer of the building, is the spirit felt by many visitors as they explore the beautiful lobby, dining and banquet rooms and hallways. This was the last of the Harvey House Hotels designed for the Fred Harvey Company. Harvey Houses had large staffs of dedicated employees who provided first-rate service. "Harvey Girls" wore distinctive black dresses and white aprons at all other Harvey Houses. Colter felt that the uniform was too severe for La Posada, so she substituted colorful aprons with green, blue or red backgrounds and featured quilted cactus, donkeys and cowboys in large Stetsons.

A former maintenance manager at La Posada came in on his day off to be the guide at our 2006 Paranormal Workshop, held at the large hotel. He escorted us to the basement tunnels beneath the hotel that led to various underground storage areas. Mark Christoph and Yvonne Parkhill felt an eerie energy presence in one of the basement rooms and felt the aura of a janitor or former maintenance man still going about his job in the basement. Several photographs were snapped in this area but merely displayed a normal array of "basement dust orbs."

Visit the eerie ballroom nicknamed the "Suicide Room," which is very peculiar and has a mysterious energy. The workshop group gathered together in the large room while two couples renewed their wedding vows. Imagine the shrieks when a clap of thunder interrupted the ceremony.

H-4224 LA POSADA, FRED HARVEY HOTEL, WINSLOW, ARIZONA

La Posada/Fred Harvey Hotel. *Courtesy of Route 66 Postcards.*

Late that night, a group of the investigators sat in a hallway and kept a vigil for any midnight ghostly visitors to La Posada. We later sat in the serene cinder block courtyard and discussed our notes and findings of the day. Members of the team thought that they heard footsteps of someone unseen walking in the area.

At the following morning breakfast in La Posada's dining room, many investigators had experiences and ghost stories of their own to share.

Debe: "My room, 110, was the scene of a suicide about a year ago. Nothing menacing happened in the room—just a sensation of always being watched."

Wendall: "It felt like some unseen presence was trying to open our room's door [room 229]."

Karen: "Talked to the tall La Posada night watchman. He said he saw a lady in a white dress in the cinder block court where we all sat talking. My room, 101, once had a guest come to the front desk asking if the room was double booked. The guest complained that an elderly lady kept wandering through the small hotel room. I also felt and heard a presence that referred to himself as Duffy."

Jim: "My wife and I shared room 211. I felt the room had a rough, negative vibration to it. She and I had a restless and troublesome night. I suffered a string of very negative dreams—enough so I woke myself up several times in an effort to stop them. I left the room at 3:00 a.m. to take pictures on the grounds. From 3:00 to 5:00 a.m., I took several pictures—one showing some nice ectoplasm. I also was able to record some EVP. I felt the EVP was not responding to my questions, but it was more like overhearing residue of conversations from the past."

Many visitors find items in their rooms moved from one location to another. Other visitors have awakened in the middle of the night thinking that they witnessed another guest in their room, only to realize that it was simply a ghostly traveler from another time.

Some of La Posada's famous guests have been Gene Autry, Bob Hope, Howard Hughes, John Wayne, President Franklin Roosevelt, Shirley Temple, Clark Gable, Albert Einstein, Gary Cooper, Amelia Earhart and James Cagney. Even though hotel personnel say that more than three hundred ghosts were "cleared" from the hotel several years ago, there seem to be many lingering behind.

One of the clerks in the lavish gift shop shared a more recent ghost tale with Colleen Sulzer of the Route 66 research crew. He told Colleen that he was rearranging the décor of the room; he had an elegant dinner place

Grand staircase at La Posada Hotel. *Author's collection.*

setting on the center table and pushed the heavy wooden chairs beneath the table. He stepped into the back room briefly to gather a few more items to display. Upon his return, not only were the dining chairs pulled out from under the wooden table, but they were also all facing the opposite direction. To his knowledge, nobody could have entered the room and rearranged the furniture in that short passage of time.

With ongoing preservation work, this treasure house of ghosts has been resurrected.

La Posada Hotel
303 East Second Street
Winslow, AZ 86047

BOJO'S GRILL & SPORTS CLUB

Bruchman's Trading Post opened in 1914 among Winslow's busy shops on Second Street. In the beginning, the trading post served members of the Navajo Nation, who bought and traded merchandise for their needs. The popular trading post was run by Robert M. Bruchman. His wife and family resided above the busy trading business. R.M. Bruchman loved the Navajo tribe and relished learning about their lives, lore and traditions. In 1923, Bruchman wrote a booklet titled *Facts About the Navajos*.

Winslow residents respected Bruchman and agreed that he was a fine gentleman and good businessman. He often smoked cigars as he worked in his office late at night, doing inventory and bookkeeping. He was also known to have a keen sense of humor. It is said that he once displayed a carcass of a supposed "Mermaid" at the trading post. He told customers that the oddity was a member of a lost Navajo tribe, and some traders actually believed him.

Bruchman's Trading Post was located on the popular Route 66 Highway and was always a stopping point for tourists who came to buy Navajo blankets and other Indian trinkets. In fact, author Debe Branning remembers stopping there in the mid-1970s to purchase a turquoise ring of Mickey Mouse. Eventually, the Navajos bought vehicles and began to shop at local supermarkets and department stores for their merchandise. The need for a trading post started to decline. Bruchman's Trading Post continued as an outlet for Navajo crafts until it closed for good in 1995.

Bojo's Grill & Sports Club. *Author's collection.*

Today, the building houses the popular BoJo's Grill & Sports Club. BoJo's provides a delicious dinner menu for Winslow locals, as well as Route 66 tourists who make the pilgrimage to stand on that famous "corner" just a block away and pose with the iconic statue of Glenn Frey of the Eagles due to the popular song "Take It Easy."

The MVD Ghostchasers led a July 2006 Paranormal Workshop at La Posada Hotel, which is a few blocks east of BoJo's Grill & Sports Club. The hungry group of ghost hunters decided to stop at BoJo's to grab dinner before the evening of paranormal investigations was about to begin. They filled the dining area of the home-style restaurant, and some of the group opted to sit in the bar area and order their dinners from the bartender.

They eagerly asked the waitresses and bartenders to share some of their ghost experiences. The staff was happy to offer personal tales of unexplained encounters with Mr. Bruchman's ghost, who they feel still oversees the activities in the building.

"We call him Grandpa," a waitress giggled. "He just gives you that warm feeling of a kind old man—like somebody's grandpa."

"And sometimes we still smell his cigar smoke," the bartender added. "We can always tell when he is around because we smell the tobacco of a fine cigar."

The kitchen staff reported hearing noises as if someone is puttering around in the kitchen. Pots and pans get moved or tossed about the kitchen prep area. They have heard their names called out or whispers in their ears.

Then they mentioned a secret door in the kitchen that leads to the underground tunnels—sweet music to any ghost hunter's ears! The small group in the bar area listened intently as the bartender educated them about the Chinese railroad workers' network of tunnels running under the city of Winslow. In many early Arizona railroad towns, the Chinese residents dug tunnels so they had a means of traveling about the neighborhoods without showing themselves on the streets after dark. The bartender pointed to a sealed trapdoor near the bar that was likely used in earlier days to move trading post items to storage below.

Workshop guest Sean volunteered to go down into the tunnels, take a few pictures and search for any paranormal activity waiting below. He was led into the kitchen, where the staff opened a locked door. He descended down a set of rickety steps that took him to a basement in total darkness. Armed with only a flashlight, Sean wandered through the catacombs, snapping photographs as he fumbled through the pitch-black pathway. He suddenly became a little unnerved and turned around, fearing that he might make a wrong turn in the labyrinth and not be able to find his way back to BoJo's kitchen. He came back upstairs and described the tunnels as being one of a kind.

The recent 2020 group of Route 66 paranormal investigators decided to have dinner at BoJo's during the research trip. Debe recapped the story of the 2006 encounter with its underground tunnels. "There was a trapdoor over by the bar. But it looks like they have retiled the floor and covered it up."

She glanced into the adjoining room, walked over and did not see any signs of a trapdoor. She decided to ask a few members of the waitstaff. They had no clue about any trapdoor or underground tunnels. In fact, one of the ladies called the current owner to verify. He acknowledged the tunnels, and the stunned waitress passed the phone over to Debe. The owner immediately invited the group to take the kitchen passageway to the basement and witness the long-lost tunnels themselves. An impromptu paranormal investigation was underway. When the boards along the basement pathway began to get a bit shaky, Chance Houston and Fallon Franzen continued into the next passageway alone.

"Keep looking up!" Debe shouted to them as she snapped more photos, "Look for the trapdoor!" And sure enough—pay dirt!

Deep in the tunnel below Bojo's Grill & Sports Club. *Author's collection.*

"We found it! It's really here!" Chance yelled from the other room. "You were right!"

The next time you are dining at BoJo's, be on the lookout for the spirit of Mr. Bruchman doing his rounds at his former trading post. There might be a hint of his cigar smoke lingering in the air, footsteps heard walking from the old living quarters above the café or the peaceful energy lingering from a Navajo trader of long ago.

Bojo's Grill & Sports Club
117 West Second Street
Winslow, AZ 86047

WINSLOW THEATER

Down the street from that famous corner in Winslow stands the old historic Rialto Theater, now known as the Winslow Theater. The building is situated between Second and First Streets on the site of the Old Bank of Winslow.

The grand Rialto Theater opened its doors in July 1927. Built by Rickards and Nace Amusements, the new theater had fine opera chairs and an air conditioning system. At a cost of about $30,000, it was hailed as one of the finest show houses in Northern Arizona. The theater featured live stage acts and later movies. It sported a Meisel & Sullivan pipe organ that was occasionally showcased until the 1950s. The theater offered silent movies until 1929, when a $20,000 sound system was installed to welcome the arrival of "talkies." The first film with full sound to play in Winslow was *Broadway Melody.*

The theater was thought to be fireproof, was two stories tall and could seat almost 650 people. The second floor toward the front of the building contained storerooms. The remainder of the building was the same height and allowed for ventilation.

A major fire damaged the theater in 1953, but it was quickly renovated, much to the delight of local movie enthusiasts. The theater business thrived once again, showing double features of big-name films. It operated sporadically until the mid-1980s. It sat boarded up off and on, and the marquee was eventually removed. New owners purchased the theater in 2016 with plans for a future reopening.

Winslow street scene postcard. *Courtesy of Route 66 Postcards.*

Several witnesses say that the ghost of a man sits in the same seat in the theater as if he were still watching a movie on the screen. Entering all alone, he takes a seat down in front—near the lower left-hand side of the theater—and "watches" vintage matinees from another time.

Managers of the theater have resided in an apartment above the theater. They often feel the presence of someone stirring about their living quarters. One couple saw a watermelon roll along the floor and across the room and then stop. Then, to their amazement, it rolled back to where it came from.

The theater is noted as having a bit of an unpleasant past. According to legend, an actress named Rose committed suicide in the theater by hanging herself from the northeast balcony in the 1930s. Apparently, the actor she was smitten with did not return the same romantic feelings toward her, so she ended her life.

The MVD Ghostchasers workshop crew had access to the basement of the theater on a stormy evening in July 2006. There is a set of stairs that leads to the catacombs under the theater backstage, behind the movie screen. The paranormal investigators explored several small dressing rooms from the old vaudeville days. The tiny wooden rooms were in sad repair and were being used for storage. One of these rooms was said to belong to the ill-fated Rose herself. Staff members have noted that Rose's

The once-thriving Winslow Theater. *Author's collection.*

sweet perfume still wafts in the air near the vicinity of her dressing room. She did not disappoint the ghost hunters. For a short time, the fragrance of roses filled the hallway near her room.

Angela Archibeque, owner of Earl's Route 66 Motor Court, told the Route 66 researchers in 2020 that while on a visit to friends who managed the theater, she looked into auditorium and saw the "ghost of Rose" walking in the aisle and holding the hands of two little spirit girls. Although it startled her to see a ghost, the spirit seemed peaceful and caused no harm.

Upon researching this chapter, no record of an actress named Rose was found in the Winslow newspapers. Could they be confusing the story with the demise of local actress Leorena Shipley? Or could the energy be Mary, a faithful moviegoer who suffered a fatal heart attack while attending a late matinee in the Rialto Theater in May 1959. It is said, "Leave the theater 'ghost light' aglow, and perhaps you will learn for yourself."

Winslow Theater
115 North Kinsley Avenue
Winslow, AZ 86047

EARL'S ROUTE 66 MOTOR COURT

Winslow newspaper archives indicate that Rex and Lillian Marble opened the doors to their motel on June 18, 1953, and proudly named it the Marble's Motel. Travel was booming, and Route 66 was the way to go!

Sadly, by the 1970s, the motor lodge, facing foreclosure, was starting to appear run-down and abandoned. Luckily, it was rescued by longtime Winslow residents Lee and Floranel Earl, who bought the business in 1974. They painstakingly went to work doing renovations and renamed the Route 66 icon "Earl's Motor Court." Their hard work paid off, and business flourished—that is, until the I-40 bypass came along and travelers stopped making the slower drive through Winslow.

Luckily, some of the other businesses the Earls owned and ran on the motel property continue to be profitable. Lee Earl operated a photography studio, and Floranel ran a busy hair salon out of rooms in the motel. Then Disney's movie *Cars* was released and resurrected a whole new interest in Route 66. Tourists began to travel the Mother Road, and families were thrilled to see the old vehicles and diners thriving once again. The Earls were inspired to restore the old neon lighting, which added to the ambiance of the historic motel units.

Floranel Earl was the daughter of Wayne Troutner, the gentleman who ran the Troutner's For Men's clothing store in downtown Winslow for many years. Early Route 66 travelers marveled over the famous twenty-foot-tall cowgirl sign that drew in shoppers to the store. Floranel operated the motel until her death in 2018.

Blas Sanchez and Angela Archibeque, also native residents of Winslow, decided to purchase the motel and continue its legacy as one of the last remaining active Route 66 motels. They found several original items in storage when they moved in, but sadly, the legendary cowgirl sign had been buried in dirt and was beyond repair. Angela replaced the outdated polyester bedspreads with beautiful handmade quilts she discovered between the mattresses of a bedroom suite she purchased for one of the rooms.

Owning the motel has a special meaning for the couple. Angela's aunt used to get her hair coiffed at Floranel's Beauty Salon, and Blas proudly owns a family portrait photographed at Lee Earl's studio in the late 1960s. To their delight, they took ownership of the motel sixty-five years after the motel first opened.

Although Angela feels that there are no malicious spirits at Earl's Route 66 Motor Court, she welcomed the 2020 research group to investigate to see

Marble's Motel. *Courtesy of Route 66 Postcards.*

Earl's Route 66 Motel. *Author's collection.*

what might be discovered. Combing through newspapers, we learned that Rex J. Marble died in a local hospital while he still operated and lived at the Marble's Motel in 1967. Could he still be watching over the establishment? And we did find a tragic tale of two little girls from the Gibbs family who died on Route 66 about thirty-eight miles east of Kingman when the family vehicle lost control and smashed into a guardrail. The Gibbs family were residents of the Marble's Motel. Do the girls still play out their last hours at their former motel home?

The group of paranormal investigators sat at a picnic table at the motel and decided to ask a few questions of the resident spirits. With digital recorders in hand, they asked if any former Route 66 travelers wanted to speak with them. They smelled cigar smoke and felt the presence of children and a Hispanic man. The strongest visitor was a woman who introduced herself as "Flo," the former owner of the motel. Investigator Chance Houston felt her presence during the spirit EVP session, and the group even heard a female giggle. Could it have been Floranel Earl? Based on the investigators' description, current owner Angela looked pleased, leaving them with the speculation that they might have a good twist on this story.

Earl's Route 66 Motor Court
512 East Third Street
Winslow, AZ 86047

CHAPTER 8
METEOR CITY

WICKED WITCH OF ROUTE 66

The original building that operated as the Meteor City Trading Post sat about six miles from the famed Barringer (or Meteor) Crater. The post took its name from the nearby landmark when it opened as a service station under the management of Joseph Sharber in 1938 for the many Route 66 motorists crisscrossing the United States.

Jack Newsum acquired the land in 1941 and added a little store so tourists could purchase food and meteor mementos when they stopped to visit the mysterious meteor crater in the desert. He proudly erected a Meteor City sign that exclaimed "Population 1" along Route 66 in July 1942. He ran the Meteor City Trading Post alone, and quite successfully, for a number of years. The popular tourist destination grew larger and featured the usual array of vacation souvenirs, jewelry and food along with being a fuel stop for travelers.

But Jack was lonely. Folks started calling him "Lonesome Jack," and after a while, he began to take it to heart. Jack decided to take a little trip to Alabama to visit family and friends, and much to everyone's surprise, he returned with a new bride, forty-one-year-old Goldie. The couple, both in their forties, never had children of their own. Together, Jack and Goldie Newsum operated the Meteor City Trading Post for almost a quarter of a century.

The abandoned Meteor City Dome. *Courtesy of Carolee Jackson.*

Jack became ill in the late 1950s and decided to resign as justice of the peace for the area. Goldie wholeheartedly took over the reins as the new justice of the peace with full approval from her husband. She was a strong God-fearing woman, and the lady tiny in stature soon became the woman many Route 66 travelers feared the most. Urban legend proclaimed Goldie as the "Wicked Witch of Route 66" due to the tough penalties and fines she handed out to speeding offenders. It was most likely a well-earned nickname handed to her by bitter traffic violators.

Jack died in December 1960, and shortly after his death, the trading post caught on fire. Goldie was forced to move into another nearby building. She and her mother continued to live and run the trading post until Goldie's death in 1967. Husband and wife are buried side by side at Winslow's Desert View Cemetery.

The trading post has gone through many changes over the years. In 1979, the building was replaced; the famous new dome design gained fame as a highway restaurant in the 1984 blockbuster movie *Starman*. This particular shop burned in 1990 and was rebuilt as curio shop for guests traveling to and from their Meteor Crater visit. Sadly, it closed in 2012. The abandoned shop became a financial nightmare for anxious business owners over the years. A huge, battered dream catcher blows in the desert breezes in front of the property—hoping for a permanent new owner. Perhaps it will be a dream come true for another pair of proprietors and the early legends of Route 66 can live on.

MYSTICAL METEOR CRATER

The Meteor Crater, one of Arizona's most visited attractions, is a meteorite impact crater located about thirty-seven miles east of Flagstaff and eighteen miles west of Winslow in the northern deserts. The Meteor Crater in Arizona is gigantic! The rim rises up 150 feet from the surrounding plain, while the hole it created is 600 feet deep and nearly one mile wide. It was created between twenty thousand and fifty thousand years ago.

The tourist mecca acquired the nickname of Meteor Crater from the nearby post office of Meteor City. The site was formerly known as Canyon Diablo Crater due to the proximity of Canyon Diablo. Scientists refer to the crater as Barringer Crater in honor of Daniel Barringer. He was the first gentleman to suggest that the depression was produced by a meteorite impact. In fact, it is one of the best-preserved meteor craters on the face of the planet.

The crater came to the attention of scientists after American settlers discovered the remote depression in the land in the late nineteenth century. Several white traders became curious when Native Americans offered their meteorite iron for trade. The settlers and traders followed them back to the crater site for an amazing discovery.

The crater was initially thought to be the remains of a volcano—not an unreasonable assumption since the San Francisco volcanic field lies only forty miles to the west near Flagstaff. It is estimated that half of the original mass vaporized on impact, and the remaining fragments were scattered across the landscape, wiping out small cactus and other vegetation.

As we know, in ancient times, strange objects in the night skies created superstitions and were often associated with gods and religious beliefs. Meteorites were misunderstood to be cast down to earth as gifts from the angels or the gods. Other sky watchers thought that the gods were bombarding the earth with displays of anger or damnation or violation of forbidden taboos.

A view of the Meteor Crater. *Courtesy of Wikimedia.*

Hopi and Navajo traditions have stated that the creation of the Barringer Crater was witnessed by many tribal ancestors of past generations. The local tribes speak of ancient folklore when a large body of fire fell from the sky and slaughtered a number of their people. "The Indians nearby have a legend about a huge star falling out the heavens and sizzling the tribe with its brightness. There was a great shock and sudden darkness, and ever since then the Indians have regarded Meteorite Mountain with awe," according to the *Journal of Astronomical History and Heritage.*

Archaeologists have discovered flint tools scattered around the crater. Early dwelling ruins were excavated along the rim. The Hopi and Navajo people gathered finely ground white silica from the crater to use in their sacred ceremonies. The white silica was sprinkled on the ground where the Native Americans danced during their sacred ghost dances. The dancers would go into deep trances where they could reunite with the ghosts of their dead ancestors on the astral plane. The "rock flour," as they called it, continues to be part of their superstitions today. They regard the meteorite as a weird phenomenon and will not disturb the fragments that lie within its vicinity so as not to enrage the gods.

Route 66 travelers of the mid-1940s found ads promoting Meteor City. The road wrapped across the hilly desert, and just three miles west of Meteor City was the Meteor Crater Observatory. Back then, admission was free and the curios were plentiful. You could buy tickets to visit the crater for twenty-five cents per person.

The Meteor Crater
I-40, Exit 233
Winslow, AZ 86047

CHAPTER 9

TWO GUNS

DESERT ZOO

As drivers head east and west on I-40, a majority of travelers have never noticed the ghost town of Two Guns eroding away in the desert just south of the busy freeway. Two Guns is about thirty miles east of Flagstaff and twenty-five miles west of Winslow, Arizona. Trapped in time—between these two cities—are the remains of what was once a popular Arizona tourist attraction between the 1930s and the 1960s.

The town was originally called Canyon Lodge since its location was near the notorious Diablo Canyon. When the National Old Trails Road was later renamed Route 66, the town's name changed as well. From that point in time, the small tourist mecca was officially renamed Two Guns. Rumors have it that Two Guns was named after a local resident nicknamed "Two Guns Miller."

Two Guns flourished in the 1940s. The tourist haven along busy Route 66 sported a gas station, café and souvenir shop and had accommodations for overnight stays. Later, a desert zoo was added to the complex with almost every beast and bird native to Arizona. Mountain lions, panthers and bobcats were housed in cages that clung to the north side of the canyon wall.

When I-40 bypassed Two Guns, its popularity slowly faded into the background. The fast, nonstop flow of traffic on the new super highway kept tourism away. The stone buildings became a part of the desert once again.

The abandoned zoo and ruins of the town sit quietly near the Old Route 66 Highway Bridge that crosses Canyon Diablo.

Nikki Wheeler, Shiela McCurdy and Debe Branning decided to explore Two Guns on a July day. They carefully followed a dirt road that led to the long-forgotten Route 66 Bridge. They stopped their truck and stepped out to examine the condition of the bridge and roadway. There were gaps on each side of the bridge where safety rails were missing. The bridge seemed very narrow by today's standards. Everyone held their breath as the truck slowly inched its way along the span of concrete.

Once across the bridge, they continued driving toward the abandoned city and wildlife zoo. A hiker was returning to his vehicle to get a bottle of water. Debe chose to chat with the gentleman and get information and the history of Two Guns. Shiela and Nikki wandered down the old narrow trails on the side of the rocky hill. They discovered the old wire animal cages from the zoo that dug into the side of the cliff. The hiker leaned on his truck, drinking his water and nibbling on a granola bar. He proceeded to tell Debe everything he knew about Two Guns, the Apache Death Cave and Canyon Diablo.

Two Guns Route 66 bridge. *Author's collection.*

Ed Randolph established a store near a 1915 bridge built to improve the National Old Trails Road. In 1921, Earl Cundiff bought the property and added the Canyon Lodge facilities. It was ideal for the cross-country travelers on the highway.

Along came Harry "Indian" Miller, who in 1926 leased a portion of the property and opened a trading post and small wildlife zoo he called Two Guns. According to Miller (aka Chief Crazy Thunder), he and Chief Joe Secakuku, who operated tourist attractions at Canyon Diablo, began building a dance floor in the Apache Cave known as the Cavern of the Chiefs. They planned to install a concrete dance floor that would measure fifteen by forty feet and attract residents of nearby communities. Harry Miller claimed that the cave, which would become a legendary tourist attraction, was created by the impact of the big meteor that fell at Meteor Mountain centuries ago. There are several cracks in the sedimentary stone in the vicinity of Canyon Lodge that radiate in every direction from the big earth fracture.

Harry "Indian" Miller, proprietor of the zoo and museum at Canyon Lodge, was bitten or mauled by the animals housed in his menagerie more often than not. There was a report of a Gila monster biting him on the face. The reptile's teeth were buried in each side of Mr. Miller's nose and upper lip. He had to tear the animal from his face, leaving seven gashes behind. On another occasion, Miller was seriously clawed by one of the zoo's mountain lions, leaving his right arm badly torn by the enraged animal as it struggled desperately to escape from a cage. Miller said that he had butchered a sheep earlier in the day and neglected to wash the blood from his hands before entering the lion's cage. The smell of blood is thought to have caused the hungry lion to spring on Miller. Another time, Miller had to seek medical attention for a badly lacerated lip, which had been torn by the teeth of his pet fox. He claimed that tourists had been teasing the little animal…or was Miller simply a careless zookeeper?

On March 3, 1926, Miller faced the deadliest charges of all. He was accused of murdering Earl M. Cundiff at Canyon Lodge. At the coroner's inquest, Miller testified that Cundiff threatened him with a revolver, and in wrestling the piece from Cundiff, it discharged, inflicting a wound on his assailant. He then shot Cundiff twice in self-defense, the wounds proving fatal.

Cundiff was postmaster as well as proprietor of the Lodge store. Mrs. Cundiff, wife of the deceased, testified that a heated argument between the two men prior to the shooting regarded property goods that Cundiff alleged Miller had stolen from his store. Harry "Indian" Miller was not happy with his lease contract, and arguments became a daily occurrence. Cundiff invited

Mountain Lion Zoo entrance at Two Guns. *Courtesy of Carolee Jackson.*

Miller to discuss this real estate matter. Miller testified that he was in his house getting dressed when Cundiff appeared at the front door. He talked with Cundiff for a time and then continued dressing. A few minutes later, Cundiff reappeared at the back door of the house and entered without knocking or speaking. Miller described the expression on Cundiff's face to be "frightening" as he grabbed a gun from the top of Miller's bureau and started toward him. Miller tried to take the gun away from Cundiff, and during the scuffle that followed, shots were fired. The jury found Miller not guilty.

Perhaps they should have heeded the Native Americans' warnings. The eerie land where Two Guns lies could be cursed. The misfortune did not end there. Miller later fought a legal battle with Earl Cundiff's widow over the property rights. This time, he lost, and by 1930, Miller had been forced to pack up and move on. Some say that it may have had something to do with the Cundiffs' store being gutted by a mysterious fire the previous year. Harry "Indian" Miller headed east, where he attempted to set up a similar zoo at a trading post in Lupton, Arizona. He died in New Mexico in 1952.

The curse seemed to continue when, in 1938, Route 66 was rerouted to the opposite side of the canyon. Louise Cundiff and her new husband were forced to rebuild everything, including the zoo, on the other side, a few yards away. It was sold in the 1950s with the rest of the property attractions, but it seemed that nobody could keep the place open for long.

Ben Dreher took the reins in the 1960s, and for a while, it looked like Two Guns might be back in action. He built a new motel, café and gift shop and reopened the zoo with a reptile exhibit. But in 1971, Dreher's hard work went up in flames in an explosive inferno, pretty much ending any dreams of keeping the attraction alive.

The hiker and Branning shook hands. He climbed into his truck and drove away, leaving the trio of gals to explore what was left of the old gas station and souvenir shop. The desert winds blew eerie whispers past their ears, confirming the disturbing emotions they felt walking the grounds of the once thriving tourist trap.

Recently, the Route 66 researchers explored Two Guns on the same pathways and posed for photos on the steps of the lookout tower, just as many bygone tourists did in the past. It is a place filled with supernatural superstition and amazing Arizona history.

Two Guns
I-40, Exit 230

APACHE DEATH CAVE

The Apache Death Cave is one of the most haunted locations along Route 66 due to its bloody history and what lurks beneath the ground. The cave is actually a series of natural caverns that extend for several miles under the brown sandstone. The cave near Two Guns is the site of a mass murder of Apaches by their Navajo enemies in the summer of 1878. Earlier, the Apaches raided two Navajo encampments along the Little Colorado River, stealing their food and supplies and killing everyone except for three girls, whom they kidnapped and made prisoners.

When the Navajo leaders learned of this latest attack, they sent out a scouting party to track the Apaches across the barren land. Their efforts failed, as the trails went cold, disappearing into the river and surrounding volcanic cinder. To their dismay, the Apache raiders seemed to slip away. While attempting to track the bloodthirsty attackers, a group of Navajo scouts noticed warm air and the smell of cooking fires, along with voices rising from a fissure in the ground. They discovered an underground cave where the Apaches were hiding. The cave was large enough to house the raiding party, their horses and the stolen goods. The Navajo warriors located the mouth of the cave hidden below in a rocky ravine. They killed two sentries guarding the entrance, dropped wood and sagebrush in the ravine and lit it on fire.

With smoke billowing into the cave entrance, the Apaches were trapped. Those who dared to escape were shot by the waiting Navajo warriors. One Apache tried to bargain for their lives, but when the Navajos learned that they had already murdered the three abducted girls, they proclaimed that the Apaches must die.

The Navajos were enraged, shooting their guns into the cave and adding more wood and brush to fuel the fire. Aware of their impending doom, the Apaches slit the throats of their horses and used the blood and what was left of their water to put out the flames. The Apaches attempted to seal off the entrance by stacking the corpses of their former steeds.

With the Navajos relentlessly stoking the fire, the Apaches were doomed to die. Smoke rose from the fissure and now carried the refrains of Apache death chants as well. When the songs faded and the smoke began to clear, the Navajos broke down the charred remains of the horse-corpse barrier and scattered bodies of the forty-two Apache warriors who had asphyxiated during the confrontation. They retrieved their stolen goods and valuables and quickly rode away in triumph.

Legend states that from that time on, no Apache has used the cave for any reason, and the Apaches would never again raid the Navajo people. Many tribes have avoided the cave, considering it and the surrounding land to be cursed.

Local tribes tried to warn would-be pioneers and settlers about the cave. It was often passed off as a legend or a silly superstition by the settlers. Pioneers who lived on the land reported hearing disembodied groans and ghostly footsteps wandering outside their rustic cabins. The stories passed down through the years of the horrific massacre at the Apache Death Cave would slowly burrow their way into their nightmares and imaginations in the darkness of the night.

Hiking down to the Apache Cave was high on the priority list for the Route 66 researchers. Armed with recording devices, cameras and walking sticks to fight off snakes, the group parked nearby and hiked up to the edge of the cliff that overlooked the cave entrance. Several of the wooden planks were missing on the makeshift bridge, and Fallon Franzen was the brave one

Hiking down to the dangerous Apache Death Cave. *Author's collection.*

to lead the way down to the dark cave. As a reminder, explorers should come equipped with a flashlight, walking stick and perhaps even a pistol to ward off aggressive snakes (or bats).

Even with the constant background noise of I-40 just north of the segment of Old Route 66, it was still a good place to meditate and feel the energy of those who met their maker in the past. Most paranormal investigators and groups that have visited Apache Death Cave say that it feels otherworldly. The energy literally draws you in—like the darkness swallows sound.

Fallon reflected, "I physically heard and felt the emotional pain and fear. The closer I came to the entrance, the harder it was to breathe and the quieter it got."

Fact or legend, the Apache Death Cave fills today's explorers with the emotions of those who inhabited the land in bygone years, and it is highly recommended as a spiritual site.

CHAPTER 10

WINONA

WALNUT CANYON "GHOST BRIDGE"

Winona, Arizona, is a small, quiet railroad town just east of Flagstaff. Once a key road stop along the Old Route 66, it easily musters an eerie feeling while you stand on the permanently closed Route 66 Walnut Canyon Bridge. The abandoned truss bridge spans Walnut Canyon and crosses Walnut Creek just one mile northwest of Winona. Soon after its completion in 1924, the road and bridge became a part of Route 66. The abandoned stretch of highway once carried weary travelers to the cooler temperatures of Flagstaff after beating the heat and wind of the Arizona desert. One can imagine the sight of vintage cars crossing the old narrow "ghost" bridge. The National Park Service listed the Walnut Canyon Bridge in the National Register of Historic Places in 1988.

Winona has ghosts associated with early railroad transportation too. The railroad runs parallel with Old Route 66 in many locations. A terrible rear-end collision occurred as a result of a misunderstanding. At 7:45 a.m. on Thursday, December 16, 1909, the Chicago Santa Fe Limited no. 4 ran into the rear end of an Overland no. 8 passenger train. The westbound no. 3 train, running late, was instructed to pull off to the side rail at Winona so that the eastbound trains, no. 8 and no. 4, could pass through without delay. The no. 8 and no. 4, both on time, had orders to pass the no. 3 at that point. Owing to time lost by no. 3 between Winslow and Winona, the no. 8

The historic Walnut Canyon Route 66 Bridge near Winona. *Author's collection.*

was the first train to arrive and stopped on the main line near the cast end of the switch to wait for no. 3. Shortly after, no. 4, following, crashed into the end of no. 8. It was reported that the flagman on no. 8 failed to go back far enough to warn no. 4. Whether because of slippery rails or too much momentum for the brakes to work effectively, the engineer of no. 4 was unable to stop at a safe distance.

The rear coach on no. 8 was demolished. Nearly half the injured passengers were from the following train. As a result of the crash, one person was killed and eighteen passengers were hurt. Alice D. Bennet of Hartford, Connecticut, who had been visiting relatives in San Francisco, died from her severe wounds. Bennett was in the dressing room in the front end of the coach at the time of the collision and was crushed in the car. Other travelers and train crew suffered scalp wounds, cuts and bruises, broken noses, wrenched backs and leg injuries.

Bennett's body was promptly removed from the wreckage and carried inside the Winona station, interfering with the coroner's investigation. There being no suitable accommodation for the body at the Winona, she was placed in the baggage car of the no. 8 and brought to Angel, where an inquest was held and the remains prepared for shipment to her home in Connecticut. The wounded passengers were taken back to Winslow, treated and released in a few hours.

A rigorous investigation of the accident was made. It was also noted that Bennett had been carrying a good sum of money on her person before the wreck. A telegram from her sister informed the coroner jury where it could be found. Sixty dollars were sewn up in her shirt, and a ten-dollar gold piece was found in an interior bodice pocket. A valuable watch was missing. The coroner verdict stated that her death was caused by the carelessness on the part of the Atchison, Topeka & Santa Fe Railway Company.

IN FEBRUARY 1927, JOHN Winchell of the local garage was called to replace a broken windshield for a Route 66 tourist's Ford. When he learned how it was broken, he marveled that the whole car was not a complete wreck and the driver not a dead man. The tourist, whose lights failed him, had driven off the Walnut Canyon Bridge and landed right side up in the bottom of the canyon. Being headed in the right direction, the man drove up the stream until he came to a place in the bank where he could drive out and seek repairs.

Other Winona accident victims were not that lucky. In November 1927, Harriet Lindley suffered internal injuries as a result of a head-on collision along the Route 66 Highway. A four-year-old Utah boy was killed one afternoon in October 1959 when he ran into the path of a westbound car on Route 66 near Winona. The family car was parked alongside the highway when the boy darted into the path of an oncoming car and suffered head trauma.

The spirits of Route 66 are said to live on along the Mother Road. Even though the Walnut Canyon Bridge is closed to auto traffic, it is worth a quick stop for photographs. You will be humming Bobby Troup's classic "Route 66," where we hear the line "Don't forget Winona"—sadly, it seems the old highway did just that.

Take I-40 east of Flagstaff. Take Exit 211. Follow the road down to the old Walnut Canyon Bridge.

CHAPTER 11
FLAGSTAFF

RIORDAN MANSION

The historic Riordan Mansion in Flagstaff, Arizona, was built in 1904 as two connected houses for two families. The two brothers, Timothy and Michael Riordan, married two sisters, Caroline and Elizabeth Metz. The sisters maintained the home, while the Riordan brothers made their fortune from the timber industry in Flagstaff. The lumber baron brothers owned the Arizona Lumber and Timber Company nearby.

The Riordan brothers built their thirteen-thousand-square-foot mansion while Arizona Territory still struggled toward statehood. The luxurious log-slab siding home consisted of two similar six-thousand-square-foot wings, one for each family, connected by a large billiard room or gathering place in the center. It is one of Arizona's most historic and elegant pioneer homes.

The couples raised their families in their private quarters, but the focus of activity each evening was in the large billiard room in the center of the living complex. The two families joined together in song, prayer, games and other forms of entertainment. At the end of the day, the families retired to their separate living areas.

Some say that the energy in the billiard room can be overwhelming. Arthur, the son of Michael and Elizabeth, had his own encounter with the supernatural when he was a young man staying in the house all alone. The families had gone off together on an outing. Arthur declined the adventure and opted to stay home for the day. Upstairs in his room, he heard the sound of pool balls clicking on the billiard table. He ran downstairs to investigate, thinking that another family member had returned home. No one was there. He shrugged his shoulders and went back upstairs. A short time later, the phantom pool game started up again. This time, Arthur witnessed the balls in motion moving across the table, but there was still nobody in sight.

The billiard room was also a gathering place for family tragedies. On September 8, 1927, Michael's eldest son, Arthur, and Tim's youngest daughter, Anna, died within hours of each other from the complications of polio. Knowing that the disease was contagious in that era, the Riordans held the joint funeral in the billiard room. The two families and the priest were the only mourners in attendance. The family was very religious and kept a miniature chapel on the second floor of the home. A legend mentions that the Riordans always kept a light burning in the chapel. It mysteriously went dark at the moment of Caroline's death in 1943.

Riordan Mansion is now part of the Arizona State Park system, and portions of the home are open for guided tours. The Riordan family donated the home and everything in it to the park for a museum of early Arizona family living. The Riordan Mansion State Historic Park stands tucked away

The Riordan Mansion was built in 1904. *Courtesy of Pinterest/Mansions Arizona.*

among the Ponderosa pines of Kinlichi Knoll in Flagstaff, Arizona. This five-acre park borders Northern Arizona University.

Although it is not presented as a "haunted mansion" by the state park personnel, they will admit that there have been some strange happenings within the historic home from time to time. Occasionally, guests will connect with a guide who has witnessed paranormal activity on a tour or doing maintenance in the mansion. Debe Branning was lucky in that manner during an afternoon guided tour. The guide had several ghost tales to tell the tour group. Many previous guests have seen the ghost of what they believe is Caroline Riordan walking the hallways in search of Anna. Caroline lovingly cared for Anna, who died from polio at the young age of twenty-six. Debe lingered in Anna's room for a long time. Her photo and college commencement announcement still decorated the room. She was to be married, but her dreams were darkened by her illness. Branning almost expected Caroline to enter the room to check on her as she stood alone taking pictures. In the past, tour guests could do photography in hopes of capturing an apparition on film.

A portrait of Tim's eldest daughter, Mary, hangs in the living room over the fireplace. As you walk around the room, notice how her head and torso appear to turn and follow you. This painting is not supernatural, but merely an optical illusion—or is it?

Riordan Mansion State Historic Park
409 West Riordan Road
Flagstaff, AZ 86001

LOWELL OBSERVATORY

Lowell Observatory is an astronomical observatory in Flagstaff, Arizona, that was established in 1894 by Percival Lowell (1855–1916) to search for evidence of life on the planet Mars. Lowell was born in Boston, Massachusetts, and always had an interest in the stars, moons and planets in our vast solar system. When the lights from the big cities of the East began to distort the darkness of the skies, Lowell decided to move west in order to continue his research and studies of the vast universe. Flagstaff, Arizona, was the ideal location in the late 1890s, and the observatory and telescopes on Mars Hill were soon constructed.

The tomb of Percival Lowell on Mars Hill. *Author's collection.*

The observatory's original twenty-four-inch Alvan Clark telescope is still in use today for public education, but not for research. The telescope, built in 1896, was assembled in Boston by Alvan Clark and shipped to Flagstaff by train. On a recent tour of the grounds, guests stopped and explored the outside of the Clark Telescope Dome (under renovations). The dome was constructed by local Flagstaff bicycle repairmen Godfrey and Stanley Sykes around 1896.

Also located on the Mars Hill campus is the thirteen-inch Pluto Discovery Telescope, used by Clyde Tombaugh in 1930 when he discovered the dwarf planet Pluto. The guests of the tour actually climbed the thirteen steps into the Pluto Telescope Dome to see the telescope itself.

It is quite fitting that the final resting place of Lowell is atop Mars Hill. It is here where "Uncle Percy" (as the staff likes to call him) can overlook the activities of his beloved observatory. His wife, Constance, designed the extravagant mausoleum after his untimely death in 1916. The base consists of New England granite and marble, and the dome is made from cobalt blue glass tiles. Guests are able to walk down to the tomb and take a peek inside to view his tabletop burial vault.

Visitors can step inside the Rotunda Museum, which features exhibits and is used as a lecture hall. It once housed the observatory's science library. Next door is the Slipher Building, which was built in 1894 and used as resident apartments for Lowell and other scientists on the grounds.

The always-busy energy of "Uncle Percy" has been felt on the grounds of the observatory from time to time. Enjoy a day of planetary studies of the solar system in outer space, and as Phoenix Lights researcher Dr. Lynne Kitei often says, "Keep looking up!"

Lowell Observatory
1400 West Mars Hill Road
Flagstaff, AZ 86001

OLD SHANTYTOWN

Nestled in the pines is the beautiful Calvary Cemetery of Flagstaff, Arizona, founded in 1892 and known as a very historic cemetery in the area. It covers about twenty acres and is located next to Northern Arizona University. The cemetery offers a spectacular view of the San Francisco Peaks to the north.

Some of Arizona's original settlers—and founders of Flagstaff—are buried here, including the Babbitt family.

There is a prominent statue of the Sacred Heart of Jesus standing near the old entrance to the cemetery. During the 1920s, 1930s and 1940s, there was a housing project owned by the lumber mill in Flagstaff. The old housing area was known to the townsfolk as "Shantytown." Most of the poor millworkers lived in this housing project. Many residents of Shantytown were members of very religious Hispanic families. They were also often quite superstitious.

The Shantytown residents repeatedly told a ghost story about a grieving woman who had lost her baby. The legend said that her ghost flew through the dirt streets of Shantytown late at night, crying and searching for her baby.

The frightened people erected a statue of the Sacred Heart at the end of the main street to ward off the ghost of the crying lady. Later, when Shantytown was closed down, the statue was brought to Calvary Cemetery. The priest and congregation marched in a long procession to the cemetery and placed the statue near the gate. Here it has stood, protecting the cemetery ever since.

Calvary Cemetery
201 West University
Flagstaff, AZ 86001

HOTEL MONTE VISTA

The Hotel Monte Vista is one of the few American hotels built largely through public subscription. Tourism was rising with the popularity of automobiles in the 1920s, so the citizens of Flagstaff were in need of a first-class hotel to accommodate cross-country travelers and boost the local economy.

Constructed in the heart of town and along what would become Route 66, the hotel opened on January 1, 1927. A contest was held to name the four-story brick structure, and Hotel Monte Vista was selected. It was billed as a full-service hotel and bragged of its running water, flushable toilets, telephones and room service.

Many Hollywood stars whose movies were being filmed in and around the Flagstaff area were guests of the Monte Vista, so many of the rooms have been named after some of the most noteworthy celebrity guests. The list includes Humphrey Bogart, Bing Crosby, Debbie Reynolds, Michael J.

Fox, Jane Russell, Gary Cooper, Barbara Stanwyck, John Wayne, Spencer Tracy, Clark Gable, Carole Lombard, Lee Marvin, Bob Hope, Zane Grey and Esther Williams, as well as the band Air Supply, Jon Bon Jovi, Freddy Mercury and Freddie Kruger himself, Robert Englund.

Today, Hotel Monte Vista is in the National Register of Historic Places, and a continuous number of ghostly guests have been seen taking extended stays in many of the rooms. There are several ghost stories told in the Monte Vista, but a favorite tale is from a personal experience that Megan Taylor had during her visit to the landmark hotel.

Megan took her camera with her and was snapping pictures as she made a sweep of the third floor. She was continually photographing the same orb as she walked along the carpeted halls. Thinking that it was just dust (after all, we do live in Arizona), she brushed it off. Megan looked up and saw a man walking toward her in the same hallway. Not wanting to be rude, Megan stopped taking pictures. The man walked to the door of one of the rooms and was going through the motions of unlocking the door with his key. Megan said the gentleman had on tan slacks and a white polo shirt and looked as real as you or me. But instead of opening the door, this gentleman walked right straight through it.

Hotel Monte Vista opened on New Year's Day 1907. *Courtesy of Wikimedia.*

The ghostly encounter does not end there. Upon further observation, Megan said that the ghost bore an uncanny resemblance to actor Alan Ladd, and the room he entered was room 309, which just happens to be the Alan Ladd Room at Hotel Monte Vista.

One of the most popular haunting involves a rocking chair in room 305, the Bon Jovi Room. Guests report seeing an elderly woman sitting in the chair or the chair rocking, or they note that it has moved to another spot after returning from dinner or a day's outing. Nobody knows for sure if someone died in the room, but some investigators speculate that it could had been the room of Marian Behn, who did live and die on the third floor. Her daughter, Ruth, worked at the Babbitt department store in the neighboring building across the street, so it was the perfect vantage point to keep her motherly eyes on her daughter from that third-story window.

Paranormal investigator Carolee Jackson with Friends of the Other Side (FOTOS) had an encounter with Monte Vista spirits when she and her husband, Steve, stayed at Flagstaff's Hotel Monte Vista in room 305. It was her birthday gift to him. As a "sensitive" and intuitive who has interacted with the other side, Carolee was anxious for her husband to have firsthand experiences like she has had her entire life. They were not disappointed:

The first thing we did after unpacking our bags, heading out for a bite to eat and to meet up with friends was to use the EMF detector for base readings. The room was silent except in the one area near the bathroom in the window curtain. After our evening out and about Flagstaff, we retired to the room for the night. Steve used the EMF detector again for base readings and got nothing. Not even where we'd gotten them before.

I then started an EVP session with the recorder, and it wasn't long before I had somebody come through me and use my energy. At that point, I took the EMF detector in hand and the lights went on. Our visitor was using my energy to contact us. Though shy and wanting to stay by the window curtain, the visitor did give some responses to questions. Those answers were recorded and can be heard in playback.

I knew the visitor was a woman, an older woman by the lack of energy she was able to draw from me. And she wasn't sure about using Steve's energy and only reached out once to him around the back of his neck. But we both had our left arms tingle and go numb. I knew immediately the woman had died from heart failure. My husband agrees.

The responses on the recorder were as follows:

Carolee asked, "Are we being too nosey?"

Answer: "Oh, no."

Steve asked, "Do a lot of people come to see you?"

Answer: "Yeah."

Steve said hi, and Carolee followed with a hello of her own.

Answer: "Hello." (This was the most distinct reply.)

Carolee continued: "Before we went to sleep, I moved the rocking chair a couple inches from where it's sat for years. There are worn grooves in the carpet, and I moved the chair to the left of those grooves. When we woke in the morning, the rocking chair was back in place in the grooves."

Another popular ghost in the hotel is known as the "phantom bellboy," who raps on the door of room 210 and announces "Room service." When guests open the door, there is nobody there. It is said that even John Wayne saw the ghostly bellboy dressed in a brass button uniform. The hotel once employed a gentleman named James Haller, who worked as a porter during the Prohibition years and was found severely injured in the basement with a knife protruding from his head, the blade penetrating his brain. He was taken to the local hospital, where he died a few days later, a victim of an unsolved "probable homicide." The Hotel Monte Vista was said to house a speakeasy as, many establishments did in the early '30s. Was Haller delivering bootlegged liquor to hotel guests and silenced by rumrunners? Perhaps his untimely death has him still making phantom deliveries to rooms of past hotel clientele.

The team StanJan Paranormal discovered a long history of deaths in the hotel. This is not unusual for long-term tenants, travelers and salesman of the day, including a gentleman who perished in the hotel lobby on New Year's Day 1951 while listening to the Rose Bowl game—a whole new meaning to a "sudden death" finish.

Hotel Monte Vista
100 North San Francisco Street
Flagstaff, AZ 86001

ORPHEUM THEATRE

The Orpheum Theatre in Flagstaff, Arizona, was built by John Weatherford, who also owned the handsome Weatherford Hotel on the corner of Aspen

Avenue and Leroux Street. Opening in 1911, it was originally named the Majestic Opera House. The Majestic was very popular with the local citizens of Flagstaff and featured a stage, a movie screen and even a hardwood dance floor, much to their delight. Things were going great until a tragedy occurred on New Year's Eve 1915 that nearly put an end to the movie palace. Soon after the New Year's revelers had gone home, the roof and walls of the theater collapsed under the pressure of five inches of snow. Weatherford was able to rescue the projector from the ruins of the Majestic, and the silent films were moved to a temporary location.

John Weatherford rebuilt his theater and re-christened it the Orpheum. It was bigger and better and served the Flagstaff community from August 1917 until the late 1990s, when the owners left town. The building fell silent for three years. After months of extensive renovations, the Orpheum was revitalized and ready to serve the Flagstaff residents in a whole new venue as Northern Arizona's premier performing arts facility.

Folks in Flagstaff say that the Orpheum Theatre is haunted. A janitor reported seeing a shadowy figure that moved about the old balcony late one night. The theater was closed, so no one else was in the building. The man

The Orpheum Theatre opened in 1917. *Author's collection.*

94

watched as the dark shadow figured glided back and forth in the aisles of the balcony. The curious worker walked up to the balcony area to investigate, only to find that he was indeed the only living soul in the building. But who was this mysterious "balcony specter"?

The employees at the concession stand witnessed a playful ghost in the lobby as the last performance of the night was playing in the theater auditorium. A roll of paper towels hanging on a dispenser on the wall began to unravel onto the concession area floor. One of them was brave enough to stop it, but as soon as he let go, the paper towels continued to unroll at an even faster pace.

Employees and theater patrons also report hearing unexplained footsteps moving across the lobby floor and unusual phenomena in the men's restroom. They have felt cold chills, electric pulsations and an all-over uneasy feeling while in the restroom. One night after the theater was closed, the after-hours crew could hear all of the toilets flushing, and the sinks started running at full blast. Was this a plumbing or electrical malfunction, or was this their prankster ghost?

While theater employees cannot speculate who the ghost might be, they pointed out that there is a tiny crawlspace near the projection room at the very top of the balcony. A ladder leads to the roof and the theater marquee. Urban legend states that a man committed suicide there, but no evidence has been seen to support this rumor. Or perhaps it is just the spirit of the teenager who tripped in the darkness of the balcony in the 1940s and injured an ankle.

So grab some buttered popcorn and a soda and take a seat up in the infamous balcony. Just remember that the person wearing that distracting hat in front of you may not be there at all.

The Orpheum Theatre
15 West Aspen Avenue
Flagstaff, AZ 86001

MILLIGAN HOME

The Flagstaff Visitor Center offers a 1.5-mile walking tour of some of Flagstaff's haunted places. It is an easy walk that covers seven historic sites where a ghost hunter may encounter a spirit or two. One of the stops on the walking tour is the red brick 1904 Milligan Home, which is in the National Register of Historic Places.

The 1904 red brick Milligan Home. *Courtesy of Carolee Jackson.*

The Mulligan Home was the former residence of Judge James Curtis Milligan and his wife, Flora. They had three children: Herbert, Lawrence and Mabel. Milligan was a Flagstaff justice of the peace and owner of a local brickyard company that supplied bricks for many of the historical buildings in Flagstaff. The two-story Milligan brick home was later utilized as boardinghouse apartments and, most recently, as the offices of the Flagstaff Convention and Visitors Bureau.

Past tenants of the apartment house and former employees of the CVB often speak of strange or unexplained paranormal events they have witnessed, including an unsettled spirit that roams an upstairs office late at night. One former employee believes that the office might have been the bedroom of former schoolteacher Mabel Milligan.

The dedicated teacher graduated from the Las Vegas, New Mexico Seminary in 1892. She taught at the Spanish Mission School in Albuquerque for several years before going to Chicago for her postgraduate courses. Mable was also a graduate of the State Teachers College of Greeley, Colorado, and specialized in teaching kindergarten classes. She taught school in Florence, Denver, Trinidad and other towns in Colorado. In 1918, Mable moved to

Flagstaff to help take care of her elderly parents. She taught first grade at nearby Emerson Elementary School for the next five years.

Mabel's health suddenly declined in the autumn of 1923. The frail, dedicated teacher taught school for as long as her health would allow her. She checked into Mercy Hospital, where she sadly died on November 8, 1923, in a diabetic coma. She was buried at the GAR Cemetery in Flagstaff.

Visitors to the Milligan Home often report hearing footsteps late at night on the staircase and across the old wooden floors. Often the sounds are followed by a freezing-cold chill and an eerie feeling of being watched. A quick check finds the doors securely locked, so no one could possibly enter the building. The spirit takes pleasure of being in charge of the CVB kitchen. A former employee recalled placing three separate coffeemakers in the kitchen area, where the appliance would not work properly. The water boiled over, and coffee grounds were spilled all over the countertop. They even purchased an expensive coffee unit, but the unexplained problems continued. The staff finally rearranged the kitchen and placed the coffeemaker in a new spot, and the events finally ceased.

On the other hand, the ghost of the Milligan Home has been known to be quite helpful. An employee came to the visitor center to prepare for an evening event. She decided to go to the back office and complete some

"Ghost of Mabel Milligan." *Courtesy of Mural Mice Universal.*

last-minute work on the computer. Somehow, she lost track of the time. She felt that cold, eerie feeling and heard something moving in the hallway. She walked out into the hall to investigate the sounds but found nobody in the building. After returning to her office, she found a picture of the visitor center lying face-up on her keyboard. The spirit simply wanted to remind her of her event and that she needed to get moving into action.

Mabel Milligan's spirit is friendly and wants to keep the house organized, just as a good schoolteacher would. A ghostly mural of Mabel ascending the staircase was added to the Milligan Home in 2016. The supernatural mural was designed and painted by Mural Mice artists R.E. Wall and Margaret Dewar.

Stop at the Milligan Home as you make your way along the Flagstaff Haunted Places walk and you just might feel a chilling breeze in the house. Don't be alarmed—it is only Mabel Milligan welcoming you to her home.

Milligan Home
323 West Aspen Avenue
Flagstaff, AZ 86001

WEATHERFORD HOTEL

One of the most historic buildings along Old Route 66 in Flagstaff, Arizona, is the Weatherford Hotel. The hotel was originally a small building containing a general store and a residence for the Weatherford family. The Weatherfords saw a need for a large hotel in the area and started construction to expand the boarding facility. Flagstaff celebrated the new three-story addition onto the Weatherford Hotel on New Year's Day 1900. A tradition in Flagstaff since 1999 is to drop a "giant lighted pine cone" from the cupola roof of the Weatherford on New Year's Eve, which serves as the hotel's birthday celebration as well.

The Weatherford Hotel was once the social gathering place for the town of Flagstaff, and it seems that the spirits are still keeping their reservations and enjoying the atmosphere of this grand hotel.

The Weatherford's haunts are focused on room 54, where a newlywed couple are said to have had a quarrel that resulted in murder in the 1930s. The phantom couple is seen entering room 54, although it has been converted into a hotel storage and supply room so it is no longer reserved for guests. But visitors still report hearing angry voices coming from the room. When the staff responds to the disturbance, they find the room vacant.

A bootlegger who was murdered in the hotel basement is heard walking up and down the basement staircase. During a paranormal investigation, the staff escorted Debe Branning to the dark catacombs, where none of them was too eager to roam. But recently, the owners have decided to renovate the basement into another banquet area, which will be ideal for that next family celebration.

The third active area in the hotel is the Zane Grey Ballroom, which displays fine stained-glass windows and a Brunswick bar that once served a saloon in Tombstone. A ghost of a short, thin woman has been seen gliding across the room. This phenomenon has been witnessed by many guests. Some report that they see the ghostly woman darting across the room and back again.

A bartender was just finishing up his shift tending bar in the ballroom when he glanced up at an old 1908 photograph hanging on the wall. The photo highlighted the Weatherford Hotel, with early guests posing on the balcony and gathering at the grand entrance. He then saw something strange, causing every hair on the back of his neck to stand on edge. As he looked on in disbelief, the scene in the photo seemed to come alive—like watching a motion picture show. People began to move about the balcony and street. He quickly finished his closing tasks and headed out the door. It only happened that one time, and he could never explain what caused the illusion. Was it truly a paranormal phenomenon or just an overworked bartender? We may never know. The ballroom has great views of the street below, and if you are lucky, you may sight a spirit too.

The Weatherford Hotel
23 North Leroux Street
Flagstaff, AZ 86001

MUSEUM CLUB

The Museum Club was established in 1931 by Dean Eldredge, who was a big-game hunter and collector of unusual items. He offered locals a place to admire his hunting trophies and large collection of rifles and Indian artifacts. Located along Route 66, it was easy for curious travelers to stop in to see his array of strange oddities for a small fee. Later, the building was reinvented as a store, trading post and taxidermy shop. Eldredge proudly displayed his wildlife trophies and created taxidermy displays for customers.

The building was sold in 1936 to Flagstaff saddle maker Doc Williams. Williams turned the Museum Club into a popular honky-tonk roadhouse and promoted it as the largest log cabin in Arizona. It was constructed around five large Ponderosa pines that appeared to be growing out of the center of the dance floor. Guests entered the door to the club beneath the inverted trunk of a native pine tree. A mahogany bar from the 1880s graced the northwest corner of the room. Patrons were fascinated by the more than eighty-five mounted animals on display from the former taxidermy shop. Before long, the locals had nicknamed the place "The Zoo."

During the 1960s and 1970s, the roadhouse was owned by Don and Thorna Scott. Being that the building was a popular western music venue along Old Route 66, it was frequented by bands and up-and-coming country music stars who stopped and entertained on their way west to Las Vegas or Los Angeles or east to Chicago.

According to local legends, the Scotts suffered tragic and untimely deaths. They lived in an apartment above the Museum Club. In 1973, Thorna climbed near the top of the staircase but fell backward and hit her head. She lapsed into a coma and never recovered. Don became very despondent at the loss of his wife. He committed suicide by shooting himself with a .22-caliber pistol in front of the fireplace in the club lounge.

Current owners feel that the Scotts loved the Museum Club and that their spirits still haunt the building. The ghostly couple mingles with patrons and the taxidermy animals when the Zoo is busy and music is playing. The staff—or "zoo keepers," as they are called—report hearing footsteps and creaks coming from the upstairs apartment. A caretaker who lived temporarily in the upstairs apartment stated that he was once pinned to the ground by an unseen force. A woman's voice told him, "You only need to fear the living." The man left immediately and never returned.

Thorna's spirit has been observed gazing down into the roadhouse from the back stairway. Other guests have seen her enjoying the music while sitting alone at a table in a dark corner booth. Men have stopped at the bar to order the mystery woman a drink. Returning to the table with drinks in hand, they discover that the lady has vanished into thin air.

Bartenders have arrived for their shift to find the shelves behind the bar in total disarray. Bottles and drink mixes had been moved around, and others had been completely knocked over. The sound of clinking glass is heard as they go about their routine of gathering their supplies in the stockroom.

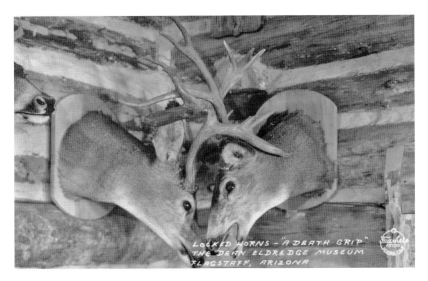

Taxidermy deer at the Museum Club. *Courtesy of Route 66 Postcards.*

Lightbulbs in the women's bathroom become unscrewed and turn off, frightening the female patrons in a suddenly dark room. The second stall door from the end slammed shut three times while a bartender was at the sink washing her hands. Other women have been pushed or had their hair pulled by an unseen entity.

Staff members have witnessed a rocking chair near the lobby fireplace moving as if someone were seated in the rocker. One employee returned after closing to pick up a forgotten item and saw the chair gently rocking in the dark near the hearth. The frightened worker ran out of the building as fast as he could.

Debe Branning was in Flagstaff on business and asked friends to join her for dinner at the Museum Club. They found a table near the backbar area just in case the phantom lady bartender was on duty. They ordered dinner and wandered through the restaurant, photographing some of the active paranormal areas.

"Fires have lit up in the hearth of the fireplace when no one is around," Debe told her friends, snapping another photo. As the fireplace is a wood-burning device, hot embers could easily reignite the wood into a warm fire again. Her nervous friends took two steps back just as a precaution.

One of the current owners described his own disturbing evening near the stone fireplace. After just acquiring the business, he planned to spend the first night there alone—a tradition he followed to make himself one with

The Museum Club is still a popular music venue. *Author's collection.*

the building. His buddies locked him in while he placed a sleeping bag on an air mattress in front of the fire's embers. Getting cold, he stoked the fire and turned around only to find the front doors wide open with the dead bolt sticking out! Was that Don Scott's way of reassuring him that he'd be around to help keep the place safe?

Drivers along Old Route 66 have glanced over at the Museum Club and observed lights blinking on and off through the windows after closing hours. Spirits still welcome the departed musicians and guests who return for evenings of dinner, drinking and dancing—an Arizona icon where you can still get your kicks on Route 66!

The Museum Club
3404 East Route 66
Flagstaff, AZ 86004

CHAPTER 12

BELLEMONT

TERMANSEN RANCH

Bellemont is located on I-40 about twelve miles west/northwest of Flagstaff, along Route 66. One of the town's biggest claims to fame was being one of the film locations for the iconic 1969 road trip movie *Easy Rider*. In the opening credits, Billy and Wyatt (Dennis Hopper and Peter Fonda) are seen pulling up in the dark in front of a typical Route 66 gas station/motel with cabins in search for a room. The motel proprietor steps outside to take a look at the prospective guests but quickly turns away, shutting the door and flicking on the "NO VACANCY" sign as soon as he realizes that the weary travelers are bikers. The eerie, vacant Pine Breeze Motel remains frozen in time along the deserted roadway. Locals say that the Route 66 Roadhouse Bar and Grill displays the film motel's "NO VACANCY" sign near the entrance of the bar—still announcing that there are no more rooms for hippies.

Gregerzi J. Termansen was an early pioneer who lived in the Bellemont, Arizona area in 1904. Termansen spent several months during the winter on his second ranch near Los Angeles. It was there that the Denmark immigrant decided to become a spiritualist. He also ranched in Arizona and owned a nice spread on the west side of the peaks in what was called the Grand Canyon Forest Preserve Townships. His ranch lacked one element to make it a profitable place: water.

Easy Rider film location in Bellemont. *Author's collection.*

After his conversion to his new faith, he consulted the spirits regarding underground water on his ranch. They advised him that at a certain spot on the ranch, he could strike water at a depth of 140 feet. He so firmly believed the spirit advisers that he entered into a contract with J.W. Irvin and John Flynn to sink a shaft on the exact spot and to the depths indicated.

Apparently, the spirits gave him some good advice because Termansen ended up selling his land in California and worked his Arizona ranch for many years. G.J. Termansen died in Glendale, Arizona, in 1957 at the age of ninety-one.

CHAPTER 13

WILLIAMS

FRAY MARCOS HARVEY HOUSE AND TRAIN DEPOT

Route 66 was completed through Williams in 1926, and this prompted the growth of several new businesses along the popular highway. Sadly, it was this increased auto traffic that eventually shut down passenger rail service in Williams in 1968. Ironically, the entire town suffered when Williams became the very last Route 66 town in Arizona to be bypassed by I-40 on October 13, 1984.

Fred Harvey opened up his first eatery in Williams when his company took over the reins of a local restaurant that had been in service since approximately 1884. Architect Francis W. Wilson was commissioned to design the Harvey's company brand-new hotel and restaurant at the Williams train depot. It opened on March 10, 1908. It was named to honor Spanish Franciscan missionary Fray Marcos de Niza, the first European explorer of Arizona and New Mexico. This facility served as the southern depot of the Grand Canyon Railway and took care of the east–west mainline traffic of the Santa Fe Railroad for the town of Williams until 1954.

The train depot was built in the same style as neighboring Escalante in Ash Fork, but just a trifle smaller in size. Fray Marcos offered twenty-two guestrooms and ten Harvey Girl dorm rooms when it opened in 1908, and they were fitted with hot and cold water and baths. On the ground floor was a baggage room, a ladies' waiting room, a men's waiting room, a ticket

H-1891. FRAY MARCOS HOTEL, WILLIAMS, ARIZONA.

Fray Marcos Harvey House, circa 1908. *Courtesy of Route 66 Postcards.*

office, a curio room, a news room, a hotel lobby, an office and, of course, the famous dining and lunchroom facilities. The hotel and restaurant were located two hundred yards west of the depot (which was used entirely for freight services). Fray Marcos Hotel was reached by two new passenger train tracks with a brick platform in between. It was styled in the Spanish Mission design, and its gray walls looked beautiful against the green fields and trees of Williams. It is the oldest poured-concrete structure in the state of Arizona. The Williams Depot and the original Fray Marcos Hotel are listed in the National Register of Historic Places.

In the 1920s, the Harvey Company added a two-story addition with twenty-one new guestrooms. Travelers often stayed at the Fray Marcos while en route to the Grand Canyon by train or by car. A sixty-three-mile spur line to the South Rim was ready for business on September 17, 1901. A maintained roadway was completed after the Grand Canyon was designated a national park in 1919.

The Harvey Girls signed contracts that committed them to working at a location for a six-month period of time. After that, they were free to head back to their hometowns or marry a local they met on the job, but many of them renewed their contracts or transferred to another Harvey facility as an opportunity to see the country and the new frontier. Williams—being a rowdy town full of railroad men, cowboys and workers in lumber mills, in contrast to the Fray Marcos—was a beautiful sight to see. The refined Harvey Girls were eager to serve this rugged bunch of Arizona pioneers. Historians often praise the Harvey Girls as being a big part of the blazing spirit of the Old West.

The Harvey staff of the Fray Marcos lived above the kitchen, on the second floor of the west wing. Each Harvey Girl shared a small, comfortable room with another one of the girls. Their work schedules kept them very busy, and when they were off duty, there were strict chaperones to deal with. Even with a 10:00 p.m. curfew, many of the girls managed to meet their admirers and future husbands and invented ways to divert the chaperones. On their days off, the girls made use of railway passes to visit the Grand Canyon and other Arizona cities. They visited friends and traveled the vast lands of Northern Arizona in automobiles.

The Harvey Girls at the Fray Marcos kept the lunchroom counter and dining room tables spotless and ready for the next train arrival at all times. When the staff was not serving hungry travelers, they polished the silver, cleaned the sparkling glasses and kept the famous Fred Harvey coffee brewing.

One former Harvey Girl recalled her first day of working at Fray Marcos. "I received nine boxes of candy from several of the engineers, firemen, brakemen, switchmen, shop men, car men and mechanics that were seeking a date or hoping to find a wife to end their loneliness."

"Working for Fred Harvey was wonderful," a Harvey employee noted, "They treated you like you were the family. They took care of you." Another one of the Harvey Girls noted, "The Harvey chain paid well and they had good living and working conditions. The food was good with generous proportions and you never were embarrassed to serve a meal."

Today, the building that housed the Fray Marcos depot restaurant and hotel is the busy Grand Canyon Railway ticket counter, museum and gift shop. It is still a "must see" location for travelers along Route 66 and visitors to the Grand Canyon. Furnishings in the depot and gift shop offer a vintage look at early train travel. The fireplace, which was once part of the lobby and dining area, continues to be the focal point of the gift shop.

The hotel rooms where tired travelers once slept are now used for offices and storage space. Seeing that Fray Marcos was such a favorite place of employment, it is not surprising that some of the Harvey staff would remain behind on the property. According to the current-day staff, it is believed that one of the Harvey Girls may still be on duty at the old Harvey House. Many of the employees have witnessed her presence.

Williams Train Depot. *Courtesy of Chance Houston.*

In a recent interview (available in *Grand Canyon Ghost Stories*, 2012), one of the cashiers had a story to share: "We call her Clara. I have not seen her myself, but I have felt her presence in the late afternoon or early evening when nobody else is in the shop. You can see something move out of the corner of your eye—or hear a movement from the back of the room, and then you just nod and acknowledge Clara. We feel Clara senses we are getting ready to close shop for the night and she is just tidying up the old Harvey House, too."

Other gift shop staffers believe that spirits like to play games and rearrange books and souvenir items on shelves and display counters. Cashiers have heard the light footsteps of a woman's shoes clicking along the original tile floors as they count out the end-of-day receipt drawers. Expecting to see a customer who was left behind or another fellow employee, they are dumbfounded to discover the depot completely empty.

A clerk at the Grand Canyon Railway counter saw the spirit of a young woman lingering near the doorway. The vision of the smiling ghost lasted a few seconds and then faded away. The counter clerk described the ghost as "resembling a Harvey Girl dressed in a uniform like she had seen in the museum's photograph collection."

Staircase to Harvey House rooms at the Fray Marcos Hotel. *Author's collection.*

Maintenance workers often hesitate before going up the staircase to the second floor, where the Grand Canyon Railway offices and cleaning supply storage rooms are now located. Startled staff members have seen the black-and-white uniformed ghost of "Harvey Girl Clara" standing near the top of the second-floor stairway. They refuse to go upstairs alone. They are reminded that the second floor was the old Harvey Girl dormitory, where the girls socialized with one another at the end of a long day. Perhaps Clara's ghost is merely dashing downstairs to greet the next breakfast train when she accidently bumps into the unsuspecting maintenance crew working in this realm.

Although the name of the Grand Canyon Railway ghost has not been verified, it could very well be the former Harvey Girl known only as Clara. Staff members agree that there was once indeed a Harvey Girl at the Fray Marcos by the name of Clara in the 1920s and 1930s. Clara's spirit may simply be a dedicated Harvey Girl who loved her job and still enjoys the afterlife perks of the Fred Harvey franchise.

Williams Station
Grand Canyon Railway
201–267 Fray Marcus Drive
Williams, AZ 86046

Twisters Soda Fountain

Twisters Soda Fountain occupies a building that was once a bustling Texaco Gas Station and motorist garage. Vacationers traveling along Route 66 frequently stopped in to fill up at the full-service station. Just about the same time Williams and Route 66 were bypassed by I-40 in the 1980s, the era of full-service gas stations came to an end as well. The welcoming bell that summoned a full-service gas station attendant to your car fell silent.

The abandoned gas station did not stay empty long. The building was refurbished and now services hungry Route 66 travelers as an old-fashioned '50s diner—perfect for visitors to Williams and the Grand Canyon. Twisters Soda Fountain is still a family owned and operated business in Williams, Arizona. The décor takes guests back to the 1950s malt shop era down to the black-and-white tiled floors, red-and-white booths and the chrome-trimmed tables and chairs. The diner offers Coca-Cola drink flavors such as vanilla, cherry, chocolate and more. It also offers ice cream treats such as old-fashioned ice cream sodas, banana splits, hot fudge sundaes and good old Route 66 Beer floats! Cruisers can enjoy lunch or dinner in a café that features all of the 1950s favorites such as Route 66 Charbroiled Burgers, Elvis Hot Dogs and Fries, James Dean Pulled Pork and onion rings.

Twisters Soda Fountain. *Courtesy of Chance Houston.*

The most compelling ghost story occurred soon after the owners of the soda fountain completed their renovations of the diner in 2008. They installed the most up-to-date surveillance alarm system throughout the café, one that could be monitored from their home. Nothing ever activated the motion sensor cameras until October 2008. An alert triggered the alarm at about 3:01 a.m., and what Jason Moore observed simply baffled him and his employees.

They watched in disbelief as a white cloudy mist eventually transformed into a shadowy human form—slowly walking through a small hallway in a back area of the diner. The audio/video recording was played over and over as the owners tried to come up with a reasonable explanation. Local TV news channels featured the video as an unsolved ghostly occurrence during the Halloween season. The strange phenomenon only happened on that one occasion. It has never triggered the alarms inside the diner again.

There have been a few other reports of paranormal activity observed at Twisters Soda Fountain. Employees note that items have fallen off shelves for no reason. One of the owners was balancing the books in the early morning hours when she distinctly heard a man inside the building say hello. The voice startled the auditor, and she conducted a thorough search of the diner. Much to her relief, there was no intruder. Perhaps it was just the mysterious spirit's way of greeting her.

Several paranormal teams in Arizona have come to Williams to organize their own investigations at Twisters Soda Fountain. The groups monitor the building by setting up night-vision cameras, trying to reenact the phenomenon that had been captured on tape. Some people speculate that the spirit could be the former owner of the Texaco Station back in the '50s. Clial T. Godwin—or "Shorty," as he was known—was rumored to have committed suicide within the walls of the gas station.

Research by Debe Branning and the MVD Ghostchasers show that he did commit suicide, but about eighteen miles west of the town of Seligman and about one hundred yards off highway Route 66. The distraught middle-aged gentleman ran a hose into a slightly opened window of the car from the exhaust pipe to end his grim story. Could this be the reason the apparition discovered in Twisters Soda Fountain takes on the form of a misty vapor?

Twisters Soda Fountain is also known for live music, vintage car shows and perhaps some full-service care from its very own ghostly station attendant.

Twisters Soda Fountain
417 East Route 66
Williams, Arizona 86046

SULTANA BAR

Located in Williams, Arizona, along Old Route 66, the famous Sultana Bar claims to have the longest-operating liquor license in the state of Arizona. The historic property sits proudly on the southwest corner of Third Street and Bill Williams Avenue (Old Route 66). Grand Canyon Railway visitors, road trippers and Route 66 explorers often stop in to mingle with the locals, enjoy a sandwich or burger and belly up to the full-service bar.

This 1912 block building once housed a saloon, billiard hall and silent movie theater. The large building boasted a six-hundred-seat theater, four large storerooms and a huge assembly room west of the theater. During the Prohibition years, the Sultana Bar provided liquor and gambling for patrons by invitation only. It was once the social center for the town of Williams—

it even housed a few of the city offices. The first "talkie" movie show in Northern Arizona premiered at the Sultana Theatre in 1930.

In the rear of the saloon, camouflaged by a janitor's broom closet, you will find a wooden trapdoor that leads down into a web of tunnels constructed by the Chinese railway workers as the railroad town developed back in 1882. During Prohibition, these passageways were used for running and storing booze at a time when just mentioning the word *alcohol* was nearly a crime. These dark tunnels were rumored to have harbored outlaws on the run. They were also known to house dingy opium dens and allegedly led to nearby brothels or speakeasies. The tunnels stretched underneath the bar and crisscrossed under the downtown area between Fifth Street and First Street.

Williams was a busy ranching town, and cowboys frequently patronized the Sultana. Arguments were often settled with fistfights and gunfire, with the most intense incident occurring on April 15, 1947, in the remodeled Sultana Buffet, which maintained an entrance off Third Street.

A twenty-two-year-old gas station attendant, Lee Skinner, had been drinking heavily at the Sultana much of the evening with a few friends and began abusing other patrons. The bar owner asked him to leave, but Skinner refused. The local law officers were summoned, and again Skinner resisted arrest. Marshal Joseph A. McDaniel was called to the scene. He entered the side door and found Skinner and his friends sitting in a booth in the rear of the Sultana Buffet.

McDaniel walked up to him and said, "Skinner, we have a warrant for your arrest for resisting an officer." When Skinner refused to budge, McDaniel reached in and began to drag him out of the booth. A struggle ensued, and both men fell to the floor, with Skinner underneath. McDaniel was shot five times with a small-caliber automatic pistol as they wrestled on the floor. Three bullets struck him in the shoulder, one went into the abdomen and one bullet went straight to the heart. The marshal was rushed to a Williams hospital, where he died shortly after arrival.

Skinner was immediately arrested and handcuffed. He was convicted of second-degree murder and deadly assault and was sentenced to thirty-five years in prison. Joseph A. McDaniel was buried with full military honors at the Mountain View Cemetery in Williams.

Many people in Williams compared the tragic crime to one committed on May 31, 1919, when Victor H. Melick was killed by Simplicio Torrez. At that time, Melick was county constable and was called in to arrest Torrez, who was wanted for robbery and horse stealing. Shots were fired,

Sultana Bar. *Courtesy of Chance Houston.*

and Melick was killed in the line of duty. Both lawmen were held in high esteem by the entire community. Their deaths were found uncalled-for and a great loss to Williams.

It's no surprise that the Sultana Bar is rumored to be haunted. Bartenders in the old saloon have seen and heard things in the establishment they cannot explain. One of the female bartenders recalled an eerie confrontation with a ghost on a Super Bowl Sunday. She was busy hanging banners and ad signs on the wall when she felt someone touch her on the shoulder. She spun around, thinking it was one of the bar patrons, but nobody was near her. A short time later, one of the local guys playing pool had a similar experience.

Another female bartender reported someone whispering in her ear while she was locking up after closing hours. Bar waitstaff report being pushed lightly by an unseen entity in the main dining room. A guest noted that she saw a man dressed in World War II–era clothing walk past the supply/janitor room. Confused, she asked the bartender if someone else was working that day. He shrugged his shoulders and told her that he was the only one on duty.

Staff members, on a dare, have reported eerie encounters when exploring the basement tunnels beyond the wooden trapdoor. Former owners of the Singing Pig, a small barbecue joint that was located in the side entrance of the Sultana in recent years, escorted Debe Branning to the hidden opening in the janitor closet. Upon lifting the trapdoor, a surge of energy filled the small room. Lacking a flashlight and permission from the Sultana owner, a trip down below was aborted.

Could former bootleggers still lurk in the labyrinthine maze of tunnels and become unleashed each time an employee opens the wooden trapdoor? Perhaps someday, when these portals are sealed off for good, the old saloon will finally find peace.

The Sultana Bar
301 West Route 66
Williams, AZ 86046

SIMPLICIO TORREZ'S GHOST

Keep away from Williams after nightfall! That was the warning issued in the *Coconino Sun* newspaper dated June 4, 1920. The wraith of Simplicio Torrez, who was hanged at the state penitentiary in Florence, Arizona, on April 14, 1920, was on the rampage. Simplicio, twenty-five years old, had been serving time for the senseless death of County Constable Victor H. Melick, age fifty-one, of Williams on May 31, 1919.

Simplicio Torrez was a troubled soul early in life. He was born in Williams, Arizona, in 1895, and as a boy stole chickens, and later, a train car full of burros. His family owned saloons, pool halls and restaurants. He was a gambler—good at cards and wielding a pistol. He was in and out of jail after committing many small wrongdoings. Torrez even spent time at the insane asylum in Phoenix. Some folks thought that he was crazy—others felt that he was very skilled with lawbreaking.

Simplicio's final crime spree began when he stole a horse from the stable of Ambrose Means, who lived between Third and Fourth Streets on Grant Avenue—not far from the Sultana Saloon. State cattle inspector Ed Hamilton and Deputy Sheriff J.H. Paddack attempted to place him under arrest, but he got the drop on them and disarmed Hamilton. Paddack was unarmed. The officers talked Torrez out of a shooting and left him—going after their guns to "take him in."

Suspecting that Torrez would return to the Means stable to steal the saddle belonging to the horse, County Constable Victor Melick was called to the Means residence at about 6:15 p.m. Torrez had been seen approaching the house by Mrs. Means, who urged Melick to come indoors and wait in her parlor. Instead, Melick confronted Torrez outside, telling him that he was under arrest.

Torrez, who was well acquainted with Melick from previous arrests, answered, "I don't want to have any trouble with you!" He turned his back on Melick, drew his gun and then quickly spun around and fired three shots—two of which proved deadly. One bullet entered Melick's left breast near the heart, touching it, and passed through his lung and kidneys and finally out his back. The second shot struck his left shoulder, while the third bullet went wild. Melick managed to fire two shots at Torrez, but his aim was untrue owing to his rapidly failing strength.

Simplicio Torrez took off running down the street, dodging behind autos and buildings. But other lawmen finally caught up to him hiding in a wood-frame house near First Street and Railroad Avenue. He was ordered to come out and surrender. Instead, he dropped down and lay flat on the floor while the sheriff and his posse fired more than fifty shots into the building. They found Torrez inside with a mere flesh wound in the left shoulder and made their arrest.

Torrez would not be able to play the insanity card for his horrendous deed this time. He was found guilty of first-degree murder and later sentenced to hang. Arizona witnessed its first hanging since capital punishment was restored to the state statutes during the election in 1918. Simplicio Torrez was hanged at the state prison hanging cell in Florence at 10:04 a.m. Torrez was the thirteenth person to be executed since the state took over the county's capital punishment in 1910. Torrez went to the scaffold without a trace of fear.

Officials said that Torrez made no statement as to his guilt or innocence, but just before the black shrouded cap was fitted over his head, he was asked if there was anything he wanted to say. He replied that he "held no malice" in his heart toward anyone connected with his arrest and prosecution and that he "faced death with forgiveness for all his former foes."

Although there was a crowd outside the prison gates, the execution itself was observed by only about a dozen persons. The mother and two brothers of the condemned man waited outside to claim the body and escorted it back to Williams for burial. His hanging rope is on display at the Pinal County Historical Museum.

Two months after Simplicio's hanging, it was noted that his spirit was coming around every night after dark, visiting in the Mexican part of

Williams and threatening to shoot everyone he sees or who sees him. One night, a servant girl saw Simplicio's spirit during the absence of the family for whom she worked. She nearly died of fright and quit her employment immediately.

Those foolish men at the county attorney's office were warned that they better watch out, for Simplicio didn't love them while he was alive—there was no reason to suppose that the heat had sweetened his temper.

Visitors can pay tribute to Deputy Victor Melick at the Mountain View Cemetery in Williams, Arizona. He is located at Plot: Sec 7. The cemetery is on the west end of Williams along Old Route 66.

RED GARTER BED AND BAKERY

The celebrated Red Garter Bed and Bakery claims the reputation of being the most haunted bed-and-breakfast in the town of Williams. Westbound travelers along Route 66 (Railroad Avenue) are greeted with a life-size mannequin on the balcony posing as a "soiled dove," waving her boa in the breeze, beckoning them to stop and spend the night.

The two-story building was built by German tailor August Tetzlaff. It was constructed in 1897 along the downtown William's Saloon Row. The original keystone bearing Tetzlaff's name is still above the arched entrance to the building. Tetzlaff's establishment was designed to accommodate the needs of the cowboys, loggers and railroad men who worked and settled near the growing townsite. It has also served as a bakery, general store and a rooming house. The building boasted a saloon on the ground floor and a very popular bordello upstairs. The enterprising ladies were often seen hanging out of the windows, calling out to the gentlemen arriving on the trains or riding past the saloon. An entrance on the side of the building opened up to a steep flight of stairs nicknamed the "Cowboy's Endurance Test." The ladies would listen for the boot steps while the business-minded madam greeted the fellows at the top of the stairs to complete the financial transaction.

Longino Mora owned and operated the main floor saloon for several years. He was also known to sell bootlegged liquor goods out of the back-alley door during Prohibition and prospered quite nicely. The front of the establishment was still a popular meeting place. The bar and gaming tables were hidden away behind a partition as soft drinks were served in their place.

Mora, a former scout for the U.S. Cavalry, boasted that he had been married five times and fathered twenty-five children. His last wife, Clara, bore his last daughter, Carmina, when he was eighty years old. He died at age ninety in 1938. With his health rapidly declining, Mora committed suicide by stabbing himself in the heart with a knife. He is buried at the Williams Cemetery.

The Arizona Territory began to enforce the laws banning prostitution and gambling throughout Arizona in 1907. Local ordinances were usually manipulated to regulate laws where brothels could operate. The saloons and brothels of Williams continued to flourish through the 1930s and 1940s. Men were called away to serve in World War II, and business at the brothels slowly declined. Legend states that a distressing murder occurred on the stairs of the bordello—allegedly, one of the prostitutes stabbed her customer in the back near the top of the staircase. He tumbled down the steep stairway, the force of the fall knocking him through the doorway. The dead man lay on the sidewalk while unsuspecting citizens passed by.

One of the legendary ladies of the night associated with the Red Garter B&B is Cordelia Curbow, better known as "Big Bertha." Curbow was born in Georgia in 1881 and worked in Texas and New Mexico brothels, surfacing in Arizona in 1917. By 1923, she was running brothels in Miami, Arizona, and took up residence in the Tetzlaff building in 1924, two years before Route 66 paved its way through Williams. "Big Bertha" was a very popular madam in town, and the Red Garter proudly named room 3 after her. She passed away in New Mexico in 1955.

John Holst bought the abandoned building in 1979 and began the exhausting task of renovating the former bordello, turning it into the first-class bed-and-breakfast we know it to be today. During his research, Holst learned that the B&B has operated as a Chinese restaurant, an opium den, a general store and a boardinghouse. Traces of the Chinese operations were found in the back lot behind the building when older structures were torn down. He changed the eight upstairs rooms—one belonging to the madam and the seven others for the "girls"—into four larger rooms complete with full baths. His dedicated work led to the Red Garter's spot in the National Register of Historic Places. Red Garter has been in full operation since 1998. It is the most popular place to sleep with a ghost, whether on a Route 66 road trip or prepping for a train excursion to the Grand Canyon.

As Holst completed his extensive restoration of the 1897 building, he began to recognize every little creak and groan within the walls. He told Debe Branning that he regularly heard a loud *clunk* around 11:30 p.m., as though the heavy front door had slammed shut. Always a skeptic, Holst

The Red Garter Bed and Bakery opened in 1998. *Courtesy of Wikimedia.*

found himself jumping out of bed to take a nightly security walk through the darkened hallways and ground floor. Relieved, he found all the doors secured safe and locked. But what caused the nightly disruption?

It wasn't long before guests began reporting a ghost in room 1, "The Best Gal's Room." This room has a view of the passing trains and windows that overlook the street below. When the bordello was in operation, the rooms in the back of the building were smaller and occupied by the newer or less popular girls. The madam had her room in the center and near the parlor entry at the top of the stairs. The most popular ladies had the larger rooms with the window views—perfect for a seductive wave to draw in prospective clients.

Guests often report seeing the ghost of a young Hispanic woman looking very distraught during the middle of the night in room 1. The ghost has been nicknamed "Eva" or "Eve" and has long, flowing black hair and dark eyes. She is often seen wearing a long white gown and clutching an object in her hands that resembles a pillbox. The distressed young spirit paces the floor near the foot of the bed as though she were contemplating an important decision in her life. The guests say that she suddenly fades away and vanishes, making them ponder if it was only a nightmare.

Visitors to other rooms report that there are playful ghosts who "bounce or shake the mattresses," or they find "slight impressions of someone sitting on the edge of the bed." Many guests have been gently touched on the arm. Some have felt their hair being stroked, and one paranormal investigator said that he "felt someone tickling his mustache." A glimpse of a gentleman or cowboy is also seen from time to time. This might be the residual energy of one of the regular gentlemen stopping by to see one of the gals. Voices may travel through the transom windows in the doorframes, but how do you explain jiggling of room doorknobs or the heavy footsteps on the empty staircase where motion sensors light up on their own?

It is still a popular location for paranormal teams, such as Phoenix Arizona Paranormal Society (PAPS), to gather and investigate the upper floors. On a guy's weekend at the former brothel, PAPS captured a few KII hits along with a few EVPs. Jamie Veik recalled the recording that stood out the most was someone stating, "We're lost."

The MVD Ghostchasers recorded the sound of heavy boot steps tromping up the staircase and walking across the wooden floors, even though there were no male guests in the hotel that night. They detected the odor of a man's perspiration accompanied by the smell of stale whiskey. Shadowy figures moved about the hallways as if the ladies were dashing from room to room to serve the gentlemen. The residual energy was heavy that evening.

The Red Garter Bed and Bakery offers an array of out-of-this-world baked goods in the morning as part of your overnight stay. Guests sip their gourmet coffee and discuss the ghostly happenings witnessed during the night. Believers of the supernatural are convinced that they had a visitor in their room—nonbelievers try to come up with an explanation for phenomena that can't be explained. Always remember, life is short—eat your dessert first!

Red Garter Bed and Bakery
137 West Railroad Avenue
Williams, AZ 86046

THE HATCHET MURDER OF HAZEL JOHNSON

The Mountain Spring Ranch slaying is like one of those camp horror movies—a couple stops at a motor rest cabin in the pines, isolated from the entire world, and somehow, during the night, a murderer with an axe attacks the heroine of the tale and terrorizes the rest of the guests in the camp.

What started out to be a cross-country honeymoon trip ended up being a dead-end journey for Hazel E. Johnson, who was widowed on March 3, 1924. Hazel Paul was a pretty twenty-eight-year-old widow with a three-year-old son when she was swept off her feet by the charming personality of thirty-two-year-old World War I veteran Granville W. Johnson. He courted the lovely widow, and they soon married on February 20, 1926. Granville convinced Hazel to sell her car and purchase the Hudson for their cross-country adventure. What Hazel did not know was that her new bridegroom had purchased several life insurance policies, naming himself as the beneficiary, shortly after the ink dried on the newly signed marriage license.

The newlywed couple pulled the widow's money out of the bank, left California in their brand-new Hudson automobile and were heading to the Midwest to meet the new in-laws when they made an ill-fated stop at Mountain Spring Ranch motor camp two miles west of Williams, Arizona. The couple pulled into the tourist camp near Williams to rest up for the next leg of their journey. Each guest had a rustic cabin with an attached garage to shelter their vehicle. The cabins had bare necessities, such as a table and cots on an elevated platform. Nothing fancy, but they offered a comfortable and safe stay—or so they thought.

Hazel Johnson and her young son. *Courtesy of Find A Grave.*

The first indication that something was wrong was when a frantic Granville Johnson pounded on the door of a fellow at one o'clock in the morning raving that his wife had been murdered and could someone keep an eye on the sleepy-eyed three-year-old. Another guest was aroused, and the threesome headed to the Johnson cabin, where they found Hazel's body lying on the bed brutally slain—apparently while sleeping, as there were no signs of a struggle, and the bedcovers were over the body in a natural way. Her head and the pillow were covered with blood.

The owner of the campground was notified, and he in turned called the sheriff. The town marshal was called also, and the officers hurried to the scene of the murder. The coroner was summoned, and he arrived on the scene soon after the lawmen. An examination of the body disclosed two wounds on the head, apparently inflicted with a sharp-edged instrument. One wound was on the forehead, and the other was on the back of the head.

Johnson told the men that he had left the camp about 11:00 p.m. to drive to Williams in order to try out a new carburetor he had replaced earlier that day. He said that he returned at 1:00 a.m. and found his wife dead. Immediately, all suspicions turned toward Granville Johnson, and he was immediately placed under arrest.

The camp proprietor noted that earlier that day, Johnson asked him whether anyone slept in the camp store and whether the camp gate was kept locked at night; he even asked to be shown how the gate operated in case he wanted to wake his family and leave in the middle of the night.

The officers did a brief search and noted fresh tire tracks coming and going from the garage. Another guest described how they witnessed Johnson driving back and forth in front of the motel earlier in the day. Was he trying to add miles to the odometer to make it look like he had driven into town?

When daylight hit the camp, the officers began to search the grounds for clues to the attack. The men found a camp hatchet that had evidently been thrown from the door of the cabin where the dead woman lay. There was a mark in the soft dirt where the hatchet had struck—blade down. It bounded several feet farther and fell to one side. There were ants on one side of the blade, eating the blood. Granville Johnson apparently forgot that the bloodied weapon had his initials carved into the handle.

Johnson was convicted of the murder. He was sent to the Arizona State Penitentiary in Florence, Arizona, and sentenced to hang on the gallows in May 1928. His sentence was commuted to life imprisonment on the morning he was to be hanged. It was there he spent the rest of life, except for the time he escaped and was later captured in San Francisco after two months on the run in 1936.

It seems that Granville had earned the blessings at the penitentiary as a trusty and was working and sleeping in the back room of a gas station across from the prison. He withdrew his seventy dollars in the prison safe, gathered a few other commodities in his name and hired an accomplice to drive him to California. It was there, they say, that he lived the life of a prince—staying at the best hotels, dining out and engaging in a drinking spree that sent him into a hospital to detox. It was also there that his actions began to haunt him. Each morning, he would ask the nurses, "Did I talk in my sleep?" He made phone calls to the prison (trying to disguise his voice), asking if "all his money was tied up?" They traced his phone calls, which prompted a manhunt to a hotel in downtown San Francisco. His trusty days now behind him, Granville Johnson died at the penitentiary in 1950 and was buried at the prison cemetery grounds.

Hazel Edna Meyer Paul Johnson's body was returned to Los Angeles and buried at the family plot in Forest Lawn Memorial Park (Glendale). Hazel's mother raised her only son to adulthood. Sadly, this bride's dream of a better life was cut short in more ways than one. Does she still wander the Mountain Springs Ranch area, seeking answers to that tragic night along Old Route 66?

The Mountain Springs Ranch tourist camp was located about two miles east of Williams on Old Route 66.

CHAPTER 14
ASH FORK

THE CURSE OF ASH FORK HILL

Ash Fork began as a small town along the Atlantic & Pacific Railroad (later known as the Santa Fe Railroad) as it made its way through the Southwest in October 1882. Initially, it was merely a railroad siding named by F.W. Smith, the general superintendent of the railroad, after observing where the three forks of Ash Creek met, as well as the many surrounding ash trees growing in the area.

Before the railroad arrived, the land had been a settlement of Native Americans, who left behind pottery shards, arrowheads and petroglyphs on the nearby flagstone rocks. Traders and trappers traveled over the land, but the trails remained wild and dangerous until Lieutenant Edward F. Beale and his crew built the famous Beale Wagon Road. Modern-day highways such as Route 66 (and I-40) cross portions of the historic trail.

Businesses began to spring up in Ash Fork in 1882 with the opening of the post office and bank, while the railroad aided the success of cattle and sheep ranching. Flagstone was quarried for the construction of public buildings, churches and offices, and the railroad had an ample supply of materials to construct needed bridges.

The beautiful Fred Harvey Escalante Hotel was built in 1907 and became the pride and joy of the rough-and-tumble railroad town. It was built of steel and concrete in the Mission style. When Route 66 came through Ash Fork, the Escalante Hotel and Restaurant catered to both highway and railroad

U. S. HIGHWAY 66, WEST THROUGH
ASH FORK, ARIZONA

Ash Fork, Arizona street scene. *Courtesy of Route 66 Postcards.*

travelers. The town's economy boomed until the Mother Road acquired a much-needed divided highway through town, resulting in a loss of several storefronts and businesses.

As more and more people traveled by automobile, the Escalante Hotel lost professional connections and closed down in 1948. The railroad line was moved farther north, and the "Big Fire" of November 1977 destroyed most of the businesses. Nonetheless, some of the classic Route 66 buildings can still be seen along the Mother Road in downtown Ash Fork. I-40 was opened in 1984, bypassing the core of the town, and soon the historic Escalante Hotel was boarded up and demolished. A small monument stands in its place today.

An article written in the *Arizona Daily Sun* (Flagstaff, Arizona) by Malcolm Mackey suggests that perhaps one of the most notorious, deadly sections of Old Route 66 was Ash Fork Hill. The hill, just west of Williams, was a 6 percent downhill grade for a winding eight miles, descending 6,500 feet. It became the gut-wrenching fear for many travelers in its early days. Somehow items being transported along Ash Fork Hill would disappear, coming up missing at their final destination. Prices of produce and auto parts, including the cost of a gallon of gas, were extremely high in some locations and not others. Nobody could explain it, and truckers started joking, stating that the mysterious corridor was controlled by the "ghosts of Ash Fork Hill."

The Escalante Hotel Historical Marker. *Courtesy of Chance Houston.*

Back in the early days of Route 66, the newspapers shared stories of travelers who attempted to drive down the eight-mile winding road from Williams to Ash Fork—often nursing a broken brake rod and trying to pilot the car to the foot of the hill before losing control and running off the road near the edge of the deep canyon. Some drivers were lucky. One time, a Studebaker's front wheel collapsed, sinking the body of the machine low to the ground. Eventually, a large boulder caught it under the rear axle and stopped the car. It was all that saved the party from serious injury or instant death.

There were head-on collisions with vehicles climbing slowly up the hill, while some out-of-control drivers descended the steep road and landed in the ditches. Steering gears broke, sending the fragile autos into the bank of the narrow road.

Things didn't get any better with the upgraded vehicle models of the 1950s. One gentleman was driving down the hill in his truck when the flywheel flew apart and burst through the transmission case. Parts of the transmission case came through the floorboard of the truck's cab and struck the driver on the leg. Hitchhikers who were riding white-knuckled in the back of the truck leaped from the vehicle, with one man dying from internal injuries and a broken leg. A mother and son were not seriously injured. The truck was loaded with twenty-one tons of eggs—miraculously, the cargo was not damaged.

In 1952, blizzards caused blackouts and more head-on collisions on this road of terror for both tourists and truckers alike. Finally, the highway was reconstructed in 1954. Route 66 was tamed by a broad new road—well paved and with fewer curves. However, even the new highway seemed doomed. In 1962, a disappearing highway was observed near Ash Fork Hill when three lanes of the four-lane highway crumbled away in a mysterious cave-in.

Cursed, bad luck, folklore…or maybe just a poorly constructed highway design? We may never know, but superstitious truckers always double-check their brakes at the brake check pull-out at the top of the hill without hesitation.

CHAPTER 15
SELIGMAN

JAS. A. PITTS MERCANTILE

A simple visit to an old cemetery can tell a visitor so much about its people and historic stories. History and ghost hunting buffs are always ready to research accidents, plagues, murders and other tragedies described on grave markers.

Reading the word *murdered* on a gravestone will spark almost anyone's interest. Such is the case of Jon Drain. Jon (or "John") Drain was an old-time resident in Yavapai County who was killed in Seligman, Arizona, on Thursday, September 10, 1914, by intruders who had broken into the Jas. A. Pitts Mercantile Store on Main Street (later Route 66). The mercantile also served as the post office. It was built in 1903 and sold everything from groceries to clothes. In 1966, the canopy came down due to the widening of Route 66. In recent years, the building has been used as a variety store and an antique store.

Jon Drain was employed as the watchman in 1914 and often slept in the store. He had been out visiting some old friends and returned to the store around 9:00 p.m. As he started to enter the building, one of the burglars, who was stationed at the front door, grabbed Drain from behind and fatally stabbed him. Drain was getting up in age—about sixty years old—and could not fight the younger man off. Two deep stab wounds in the back were enough to cause his death, but it is believed that Drain died from a fractured skull caused by a blow of a heavy weapon.

The Jas. A. Pitts Mercantile Building in Seligman. *Author's collection.*

Another burglar had been drilling the safe in a most expert manner when Drain discovered the intruders. It was learned that fifty dollars in silver and eighteen six-shooters and ammunition were stolen by the thieves, who easily made their escape. Jon Drain's body was found lying on the floor near the front entrance when Postmaster Pitts opened up for business the next morning. Besides the pool of blood around his head, there were bloodstains along the floor and bloody fingerprint stains around the rear door where the murderers made their getaway.

Drain was born in Ireland and had previously lived in the nearby town of Williams, Arizona, but settled down and called Seligman home. His remains were brought to Flagstaff, where his funeral was attended by many old-time friends and family.

There was a reward of $1,500 offered for the capture of his murderers. The horrible act aroused the entire vicinity to a borderline frenzy, and there was talk of organizing a search posse. But the men realized that the criminals probably grabbed an east- or westbound train after committing their deed and were long gone.

Several months earlier, the postmaster at the time, Mr. McBride, had shot and killed a man named Edwards at the same location. Edwards threatened to break down the door if not opened. A bullet went thought the door and killed Edwards almost instantly. McBride was exonerated of the crime.

Grave of Jon Drain (1854–1914) at Calvary Cemetery, Flagstaff. *Author's collection.*

This historic (and probably most haunted) structure is one of the oldest buildings still standing in Seligman, and you can find it on the corner of Main and Old Route 66. Seligman is located about seventy-six miles west of Flagstaff, Arizona.

CHAPTER 16

PEACH SPRINGS

GRAND CANYON CAVERNS AND BUNK HOUSE

There have been several reports that the Grand Canyon Caverns—located at mile marker 115 along Route 66 near Peach Springs, Arizona—is haunted. Several of the buildings on the property, such as the Bunk House, have a few ghost tales of their own. Guests can book the Cavern Suite and sleep 220 feet below ground in the haunted cavern.

The cavern property was discovered by Walter Peck in 1927. It has also been known as Dinosaur Caverns and has seen several property owners. The old cavern's entrance led to a sacred Native American burial site, and the caverns were considered a holy place. Ladders, steps and a swinging bridge were constructed in the caverns in 1935. An elevator was installed in 1962, and the natural entrance to the cave was permanently sealed.

The most frequent ghostly vision is that of a man standing in the elevator, either at the top or the bottom of the shaft, opening and closing the doors. Caverns employees believe that he is Walter Peck. One of the paranormal claims noted is that a four-inch rock sailed horizontally through the caverns and landed near an investigator. Movement noises have been heard in the rocks near the headboards of the beds in the Cavern Suite. Noises near the wooden stairs adjacent to the suite have been heard. The sounds of rocks beating together have been heard. Tour guides have seen chains swing on their own and small shadows darting near the pathways, and there's the constant feeling of being followed. Tour guides and visitors alike have

Dinosaur Caverns' vintage billboard. *Courtesy of Route 66 Postcards.*

reported seeing strange figures and dancing shadows on the rock walls and hearing chanting and other noises. It is said that the caverns have been the scene of at least eight deaths, and another four people with strong ties to the caverns have died young in the last fifty years.

The bunkhouse is reported to have been constructed in the 1940s, with at least one or two add-on room additions since then. It was once owned by the Ringsby Trucking Company. Reportedly, General Manager Gary Ringsby hanged himself from a beam in the bunkhouse living room area in the 1970s. The bunkhouse is now used as large family sleeping quarters that can accommodate ten guests.

Past paranormal investigation claimed EMF readings at various locations of the living room, with light to medium EMF ranges. EMF meters responded to questions. Static and REM Pods went off. Other paranormal teams reported high EMF activity at 8:00 p.m. and between 11:00 p.m. and midnight.

In February 2013, five paranormal teams came together and took part in a formal investigation of the caverns and grounds. The collaborating teams were MVD Ghostchasers, the Reaper Team, LIPS, Verde Valley Spirit Seekers and Arizona Paranormal. Using various cameras, meters and recording devices, the group divided up into two teams, which gave everyone an ample opportunity to spend time investigating each location during the course of the night. Here are the results from the bunkhouse.

Research showed that Gary Ringsby did not hang himself in the living room of the bunkhouse. A Colorado death certificate was located that indicated he died in Colorado. A newspaper clipping dated June 9, 1973, indicates that Ringsby (then thirty-six) drove to a parking lot at the Cherry Creek Reservoir, got out of his truck and shot himself in the chest with a shotgun.

EMF/EVP sessions in the bunkhouse began at 8:00 p.m. Activity was not sustained or reliable enough to indicate a strong spiritual presence. An external survey of the bunkhouse revealed loose wiring and water leaks in the plumbing system. Several of the residents on the cavern property used external generators, which could have caused interference. Without further investigation, the five teams concluded that the bunkhouse was not haunted by a strong spirit—or perhaps the spirits were just not active on the night of their visit.

The Arizona paranormal team FOTOS spent the night in the large bunkhouse. The group stood in the kitchen area, opening the coolers and munchie bags. They chatted about what they experienced and vowed to return another time, as their overnight reservation to investigate the Cavern Suite below had been canceled. Reggie elected to sleep in an extra room near the dining table. Greg took a spare bedroom, while the ladies agreed to share accommodations in the bunkbeds room. The group was laughing and

Bunkhouse at Grand Canyon Caverns. *Courtesy of Chance Houston.*

talking when, suddenly, the door near the table slowly unlatched and opened about six inches. Reggie changed his mind and opted to sleep on the sofa in the living room instead.

Here are the results from the caverns: The members of the teams took a walking tour with the guide to familiarize themselves with the cave and its surroundings. Initials "PW" or "PV" were discovered on the wall in the far corner of the caves, where the guide said they were never noticed during several prior tours.

One investigator saw the shadow of something low to the ground about the size of a bobcat or small animal dart twice in the fallout shelter storage area. A second investigator, someone who is not normally sensitive to hauntings, experienced extreme fear and despair near the ladders close to the bridge (old entrance) area of the caverns. The guide escorted two investigators across the bridge and up in the ladder area to observe the old entrance to the cave. The investigator began to weep and cried out in fear over a "feeling" of someone who had died or had been seriously injured in an accident—perhaps during construction within the cavern. She believed that the name of the injured spirit was "Kevin."

A third investigator who walked the caverns most of the night from 2:00 a.m. until 4:30 a.m. reported the feeling of being watched from the fenced-off area near the "snow ball" room. He had a feeling of despair, anguish and hopelessness near the wooden bridge at the old entrance.

Another investigator saw what she believed to be a young man who was "filmy," although she could make out his features clearly, standing just inside the cavern area (near the elevator entrance) looking toward the Cavern Suite. The apparition was just standing there, watching. She and two other investigators rushed to the spot and felt a very cold energy breeze whisk past them, and then the energy of the area dissipated.

The sound of an occasional rock falling from the cavern walls broke up the stillness of the night. Investigators reported the feeling of being watched or followed on the pathways in the caverns but nothing aggressive.

Without further investigation, the five teams feel that the Grand Canyon Caverns are only active due to residual energies that are imprinted into the stone walls—or perhaps the physical spirits were not active on the night of their visit.

Grand Canyon Caverns and Bunkhouse
Mile Marker 115 Route 66
Near Peach Springs, AZ 86434

Harvey Hudspeth's Foreboding Dream

Harvey F. Hudspeth was born in Bandera County, Texas, on September 19, 1878, and resettled in the Arizona Territory in 1896. The young man entered the sheep business with his elder brother, Thomas J. Hudspeth, the president of Hudspeth Sheep Company and one of the largest sheep owners in Arizona. Harvey was known to be a genial, wholehearted man, always ready to respond to the call of those in need. He was well liked and highly respected by all.

Hudspeth was struck by Santa Fe passenger train no. 9 at Nelson, Arizona, while crossing the track in his automobile on May 2, 1921. Harvey suffered several deep cuts, a number of broken bones and internal injuries.

According to the only eyewitness of the accident (the railroad agent of Nelson), it appeared that Mr. Hudspeth left the main highway and passed through the gate entrance to the tracks; after going back and closing it, he reentered his car and started slowly across the tracks, there being three at that point. There was quite a deep cut about sixty yards east of the crossing, and one could not see an approaching train until nearly on the main line.

The train was moving down the grade swiftly and silently. A hard wind blew the sound of the oncoming locomotive in the other direction, and since Mr. Hudspeth had lost the sight in his left eye, it is thought that he did not see the train approaching from that side until it was too late to stop. He did try to turn the wheel of his car to the right in an attempt to receive the shock of the collision from the rear. Unfortunately, it was too late, and the car was struck with all the force of the onrushing train; it was hurled into the air and scattered into fragments. His body was thrown about one hundred feet, and when the train crew reached him, his life was almost gone, although his breathing continued faintly until the town of Valentine was reached. The coroner, after visiting the scene of the tragedy, brought in a verdict of accidental death.

His friends gathered at the Kingman train station, hoping that their worst fears might not be realized and that the unfortunate man might not be as badly injured as reported. Sadly, the train brought only his dead body. The waiting friends turned away, overwhelmed with grief, when his cold and lifeless form was removed from the train.

Hudspeth's funeral was held at St. John's ME Church, and he was buried at Mountain View Cemetery in Kingman.

It was recalled by several friends and associates that Harvey told them about a dream he had only a few nights before his death. He said that in his dream, he seemed to be crossing a railway track when his car was struck by a train and cut in two—but he emerged without injury. In the light of subsequent events, it seems that the dream was, for the first part, prophetic.

Had he listened to warning signals in the foreboding dream, perhaps he would have detoured and taken a different route along the old highway that day. Hudspeth held a ticket for the train of death. Does his soul still protect those approaching the railroad crossing? Listen for the train whistle in the rushing winds.

Nelson is a few miles south of Route 66 near Peach Springs.

CHAPTER 17

TRUXTON

FRONTIER MOTEL AND CAFÉ

Truxton was established in 1951 by Clyde McCune and Donald Dilts when they learned that a dam would be constructed on the Colorado River at nearby Bridge Canyon. The name Truxton was selected to honor Truxtun, the son of Lieutenant Edward F. Beale, who found a spring in the area while surveying a wagon road from Fort Smith, Arkansas, to California in 1882–83.

A service station and garage were built close to the head of Crozier Canyon, about 8.5 miles southwest of Peach Springs. Anticipating a heavy flow of trucks and autos, a café was added to the location. Although the dam was never built, the businesses thrived due to the busy Route 66 traffic. The town along the nearby railroad siding grew, and soon more new businesses such as motels, restaurants and garages flourished.

One of these new businesses, the Frontier Motel and Café, was operated by Alice Wright in the 1950s. Mildred Barker worked in the café in 1956. It was eventually sold to Ray and Mildred Barker, who took the reins in the 1970s. Mildred became quite well known in the area for her hospitality and friendly disposition. Journalist Jann Scott did a video TV series on Route 66 between 1993 and 2003. During his Truxton afternoon visit, he sat down at a table in the Frontier Café and conducted an informal interview with owner Mildred Barker. When asked, "Do you have any good ghost stories?"

Ruins of the Frontier Motel in Truxton. *Author's collection.*

Mildred smiled and didn't hesitate to answer. She noted that several Indians were killed on the Route 66 roadway when traffic was bad. Sometimes they were trying to cross the busy highway, and other times they were hit as they walked along the narrow road. The deceased spirits would leave something (perhaps energy) near the front door. She often looked at the doorway and could see what looked like an Indian standing there, as if he had been injured or run over by a vehicle. It always gave her the "Squebadees," she said, as she chuckled and gave a slight shiver.

Ray Barker passed away in 1990, but Mildred continued to run the roadside café until her death in 2012. An eerie silence hovers over the once active center of town. The colorful diner now sits decayed and deserted, while the faded neon signage can only be seen by the ghosts of the past.

Frontier Motel and Café
Route 66
Truxton, AZ 86437

CHAPTER 18

VALENTINE

TRUXTON CANYON INDIAN SCHOOL

After the United States took this territory from Mexico, the government commissioned Captain Lorenzo Sitgreaves (1810–1888) to explore what is now Valentine, Arizona, in 1851. Sitgreaves was followed by Lieutenant Edward "Ned" Fitzgerald Beale (1822–1893), who surveyed a wagon trail in 1857 in order to link Arkansas with California.

Once the local Hualapai natives were defeated and relocated to a nearby reservation, the railway built its tracks in 1882 along Beale's iconic trail through what would become the town of Valentine. The Atchison, Topeka & Santa Fe Railroad arrived in the area in 1883, and a siding was built that was called Truxton. (The town of Truxton, to the northwest, was not established until 1951.)

The settlement began with the opening of the Truxton Canyon Training School. About 660 acres were set aside, and the construction of the two-story school began in 1901. It would serve as a day school for the nearby Hualapai Indians and a boarding school for children of the Apache, Havasupai, Hopi, Mojave, Navajo and Papago tribes. During this time, education was central to the United States Indian policy, which worked to assimilate Native Americans into American culture. The school opened its doors in 1903 as an industrial training institution. Students spent some time each day in academic classes. During the rest of the hours, boys were taught a trade, while the girls learned domestic skills. Some members of the tribes were reluctant to leave their settlements and made every attempt to remain behind—even if it meant suicide.

In 1901, the town gained a post office, which was also called Truxton. But in 1910, the town and post office were renamed Valentine—after Robert G. Valentine, who proudly served as the commissioner of Indian affairs from 1909 to 1912. The National Old Trails highway passed through Valentine in the 1910s and became part of the Route 66 alignment in 1926. It provided a steady flow of travelers until it was bypassed by I-40 in 1979.

A separate red brick schoolhouse was erected for white children in 1924. It was located southeast of the Indian school and was referred to as the "Red Schoolhouse." That same year, the Indian school was expanded with bricks manufactured on site by the Hualapai students. One can recognize the informal masonry brickwork of the students as you view the structure today. Soon a dozen or more buildings stood on the school grounds. In 1937, a Hualapai day school opened in Peach Springs; this led to the closing of the Truxton Training School, and many of its buildings were destroyed. Only the two-story brick schoolhouse remains today. It is listed in the National Register of Historic Places. The Red Schoolhouse remained open for area students until 1969.

Henry P. Ewing, recognized as the "blind miner," was an erratic, well-known figure in the Valentine area. He came to this country in about 1883 and lived his days out as the assessor of the county, sheriff and deputy sheriff under various administrations. He was an industrial teacher in 1900 at the Truxton Canyon Indian School and later became the superintendent of the school. He was also an agent for the Hualapai Indians. It was in this position that he became involved in trouble with the government. He was charged with falsifying accounts to defraud the government in the amount of $1,200. Friends acknowledged that this possibly hastened the decay of his mental faculties. He became blind in 1906 but refused to live in town, preferring to remain at his mines in the Goldroad area. While at the mines, he became violently insane, accusing friends and family of poisoning him. In 1907, he was sent to the asylum near Phoenix, where he gradually grew worse. He died in 1908 and was buried at Greenwood Cemetery in Phoenix.

During Valentine's heydays, thousands of Valentine cards and messages would flood into the tiny post office for its popular heart-shaped postmark with a cupid's arrow. The post office was located on the south side of Route 66 next to what is now an abandoned Union 76 service station. Tragedy struck on the afternoon of August 15, 1990. On that hot afternoon, forty-

Abandoned Truxton Canyon Indian School. *Author's collection.*

four-year-old postmistress Jacqueline Ann Grigg was busy working when a short, stocky white man robbed the post office of $40 in cash and $800 in postal money orders. He stole her car and left Grigg dying on the floor from a gunshot wound. The man was captured and sentence to life in prison. It was not long after that Jacqueline's husband demolished the building and left the area. The Valentine postmark was retired to the Kingman Post Office, where folks can still get their special cards enhanced with the heart-shaped cancelation stamp.

This small Route 66 town seemed to carry the burden of several earlier tragedies as well. In 1907, fifty-four-year-old Michael Maguire fell behind the wheels of a freight train just a mile west of the Indian School as he was trying to hop on for a free ride. His right leg was mashed to a pulp. He was immediately brought to the Truxton Canyon Indian School to be treated. He died in Hackberry on the train en route to Kingman.

Dr. E.P. Ford was hunting rabbits in the heavy mesquite brush near the Truxton Canyon Indian School when he somehow accidently shot himself through the heart with a Winchester shotgun. His body was found some time later by his wife and children. It was presumed that he had tripped and, in falling, the gun was discharged, with the buckshot entering the body above the heart and causing instant death. Dr. Ford and his family had been at the school about five months and were favorites with the students and staff. Edwin P. Ford was only thirty-five years old and was buried at the Kingman Cemetery.

On September 13, 1924, John Light—just four years old—died at the Truxton Canyon Indian School as a result of an accidental discharge of a .22-caliber rifle. The lad had inserted a shell, and his seven-year-old brother was trying to take the gun from him when it discharged. The bullet passed through the right shoulder. He was the grandson of the superintendent of the school.

Have these heartbreaking accidental deaths of long ago trapped the spirits within the historic abandoned buildings? Look up into the weathered windows and feel the sadness of the former students, the tragedies of those who worked there. Listen to the coyotes, which mourn them all.

Truxton Canyon Training School
North side of Route 66 along Music Mountain Circle
Valentine, AZ 86437

CHAPTER 19

HACKBERRY

GIGANTICUS HEADICUS

The once thriving mining town of Hackberry dates back to 1874. The railroad came through in 1882, and the town was moved four miles from its original site and became a loading stop for cattle. A nearby silver mine earned almost $3 million before it closed in 1919, causing Hackberry to become another desert ghost town.

In 1926, Route 66 gave new life to the Hackberry General Store as a major service and supply stop. Business flourished between 1934 and the 1970s, but then, sadly, I-40 bypassed the town. Travelers abandoned the general store once again until artist Bob Waldmire reopened its doors in 1992, and it became one of the most popular stops along Arizona's original Route 66 miles. The old grocery store is filled with trinkets and treasures ideal for every Route 66 enthusiast. It is a living museum with Route 66 memorabilia, souvenirs, vintage cars and old gasoline pumps for photo opportunities. It is a perfect spot to rest or sip on a bottle of Route 66 Beer.

Travel a mere six miles west of Hackberry and you come to the tiny railroad village of Antares. It is here you will discover the fourteen-foot sculpture called *Giganticus Headicus*, which resembles a partially buried Easter Island Head. The artwork was created in 2003 and 2004 by local artist Gregg Arnold and stands among several other pieces of creative mysteries.

The *Giganticus Headicus* protects Route 66. *Author's collection.*

Giganticus Headicus is essentially a replica of the ancient stone monoliths known as Moai ("statue") that surround Easter Island in the South Pacific. Archaeologists who study the Moai suggest that they may have played an essential role in the island's road system and were left in place to watch over the people. It is also suggested that they had a religious and possibly mystic reason for their existence. The symbols could represent authority and power—both religious and political. When these objects are properly erected and ritually set up, it is believed that they are charged by a magical essence called mana.

Be sure and go inside the gift shop and get your own miniature copy of a *Giganticus Headicus* to ward off evil spirts as you continue your own travels along Route 66. And another note for you *Star Trek* fans: a local legend claims that *Star Trek* creator Gene Roddenberry paid a visit to Antares and stayed at the motel. It was there that he made the decision to name the *Antares* starship in *Star Trek* after the Route 66 location. After all, it is the fifteenth-brightest star in the night sky and represents the Scorpion's Heart in the constellation Scorpius.

Hackberry Store
Route 66
Hackberry AZ 86411

THE SUPERSTITION OF THE "WALLAPAI"

A Mohave Country newspaper out of Kingman told the following story in June 1919 concerning a superstition of the "Wallapai" (Hualapai) tribe. Sam Martin was at the camp of the Indians near Hackberry and was told that a rattlesnake had gotten into one of the nearby hogans. He asked the Indian why he had not killed the reptile and was told that it was not good luck to kill the snake at any hour other than at sunup or sundown. In fact, the fellow had watched the snake all night in fear and trembling, but his fear of the ill luck that might come to him or his tribe overweighed his desire to kill it; therefore, he and his wife and children watched its every movement so it could do no harm. At the hour of sunup, his "snakeship" was taken outside the hogan and sent away.

There are many beliefs, superstitions and phobias about the rattlesnake, and sometimes their reputation has made them misunderstood. Although they are dangerous, they do not want to bite anything unless they plan on eating it, and a human would just not fit in their mouths. Simply watch where you step and place your hands when outdoors. And as the Hualapai noted, if you should encounter one, give it plenty of space.

CHAPTER 20
KINGMAN

Kingman was founded in 1882, when Arizona was still considered the Arizona Territory. Situated in the Hualapai Valley between the Cerbat and Hualapai Mountain Ranges, Kingman began as a simple railroad siding near Beale's Springs in the Middleton Section along the Atlantic & Pacific Railroad. Kingman was named for Lewis Kingman, who surveyed along the Atlantic & Pacific Railroad's right-of-way between Needles, California, and Albuquerque, New Mexico. Lewis Kingman supervised the building of the railroad from Winslow to Beale's Springs, which is near the present location of Kingman.

There is a marker in Kingman that indicates the area of the Beale's wagon trail, which became the dusty National Old Trails Highway and, later, in 1926 became a valued segment of the famed Route 66. Driving through town is like going back in time. Check out the Route 66–themed motels, restaurants, shops and museums and be transported to what life on the Mother Road was really like.

During World War II, Kingman was the site of an U.S. Army Air Force airfield. The Kingman Army Airfield was founded at the beginning of the war as an aerial gunnery training base for thirty-five thousand soldiers and airmen. Following the war, the Kingman Airfield served as one of the largest and best-known reclamation sites for obsolete military aircraft.

After the war, Kingman experienced growth as several major employers moved into the vicinity. In 1955, Ford Motor Company established an auto testing/proving ground. Several major new neighborhoods in Kingman were developed to house the skilled workers and professionals employed at the proving ground, as Kingman was the only large developed town within the area. About this same time, the development of the Duval copper mine near Chloride, Arizona, and construction of the Mohave Generating Station in Laughlin, Nevada, began and contributed to Kingman's population growth.

Actor Andy Devine (1905–1977) was raised in Kingman, where his father operated the popular Beale Hotel along Route 66 and across the road near the railroad station. The Old Route 66 thoroughfare is now named "Andy Devine Avenue," and the town celebrates the annual "Andy Devine Days" each September.

HOTEL BRUNSWICK

The Hotel Brunswick, built in 1909, was one of the first three-story buildings in the Kingman, Arizona area. Legend says that a rivalry between the hotel's early owners, Mulligan and Thompson, divided the hotel in two separate businesses. One half of the brick building operated as a hotel/restaurant, while the other half was run as a hotel/saloon. Nevertheless, both proprietors were quite successful.

The Hotel Brunswick is also known to be haunted. Mysterious coins have appeared out of nowhere in hidden corners of the hallways and the lobby. Guests report strange appearances of apparitions or sense ghostly presences in their rooms tucking them in or touching their heads or feet. A male ghost has been seen coming up the cellar steps.

Could one of the ghosts haunting the Brunswick be due to the sudden death of William D. McCright? Mr. McCright, about seventy-four years old, was found dead in his room at the Hotel Brunswick on March 7, 1915. The elderly man's death came without warning and seemed to be of natural causes. He had apparently risen out of his bed at the usual hour and was making his morning ablutions when the grim terror called him out. Not making his morning appearance downstairs for breakfast, Mr. Miller went up to his room and found the gentleman lying on the floor dead, clutching a towel in his hands.

Born in Pennsylvania in 1841, McCright first came to Arizona from the California coast in 1874. He arrived in Kingman about 1913 and moved into the upscale Hotel Brunswick. He usually woke up about 7:00 a.m., ate breakfast and then whiled away the day reading and talking about old times with friends. His fondness for and knowledge of the Pacific coast area earned

The historic Hotel Brunswick was built in 1909. *Author's collection.*

him many fast acquaintances. His colleagues loved hearing his tales of early Arizona. McCright settled in Signal, Arizona (now a ghost town), where he resided for forty years. He was one of the owners of a large mining property known as the McCracken mines and received a large sum of money when he sold his interest in the mining business.

The retired miner spent the last years of his life as a resident of the Brunswick. His acquaintances stated that he was a good-hearted man and always there to help a friend. Is he the spirit that leaves the coins scattered about the hotel in times of need? He was buried at the historic Mountain View Cemetery in Kingman, near and dear to the untamed land he loved.

The Mulligan family sold the hotel in 1928, and there have been several additional owners over the years. One of the more recent owners reported smelling the scent of lilacs, which she interpreted as being Sarah Mulligan, one of the members of the family. They also heard the scampering of children's footsteps throughout the building and playful giggles.

Hotel Brunswick is closed for business at this time, but you can never know when the next entrepreneur will come along and resurrect it.

Hotel Brunswick
315 East Andy Devine Avenue
Kingman, AZ 86401

LEE WILLIAMS HIGH SCHOOL

Lee Williams High School is the second comprehensive high school in the town of Kingman, Arizona. It opened on August 9, 2012, one year later than originally planned. It is named for Richard Lee Williams, a former school principal and firefighter who died while fighting the Doxol disaster in 1973. The catastrophe was due to a boiling liquid expanding vapor explosion that occurred during a propane transfer from a Doxol railroad car to a storage tank on the Getz rail siding near Andy Devine Avenue/Route 66. The school's team name is the Volunteers.

The football stadium at the school gives an entirely different meaning to the phrase "team spirit." This football field was built on what was once the Pioneer Cemetery of Kingman. The Pioneer Cemetery was the original cemetery in Kingman and accepted burials from 1900 to 1917. It was the final resting place for more than four hundred Mohave Country pioneers from Kingman and surrounding communities.

As the population of Kingman grew in the early 1900s, the search for real estate to expand became vital to businesses, families and investors. By 1917, the town was in need of a high school to meet the educational requirements for Kingman's students. The land where the old cemetery was laid out looked like the ideal central location. Mohave County donated the old Pioneer Cemetery property to the school board to build a new high school. A stadium and parking lot replaced the hallowed grounds. Oddly, the historic cemetery had been moved twice before—from one side of the railroad tracks to the other. It was thought that the cemetery was finally allotted a permanent location—the site of the present-day high school and the adjacent parking lots at the Lee Williams Stadium.

Sometime around 1917, the county began the task of moving the graves of the dearly departed to the new Mountain View Cemetery a few miles away. Mohave County did not pay for loved ones to be moved to the new cemetery. That was the family's responsibility. Some burials were not removed due to faulty recordkeeping or lack of gravestone markers to identify bodies. So, some of the not-so-dearly-departed, whose relatives did not come forward, were not moved and were instead left behind at the deserted cemetery with a few stones standing in place.

Mohave Union High School opened its doors at this site in late 1917 on the corner of Fourth Street and Oak Street in downtown Kingman. In 1944, the cemetery land was about to be repurposed once again because of the need for a junior high school. Mohave County offered to try to relocate the

Kingman Pioneer Cemetery Memorial. *Courtesy of Hollie Hickle.*

existing burial plots and bodies to the newer cemetery. Sadly, it was charging $45 per person to remove the remains (which in 1944 was equivalent to $600 by today's standards). Many families could not afford those prices, and as a result, many of the bodies again remained unclaimed.

They say that in the 1940s, a group of youngsters playing on the football field began to unearth bones of the bodies that were never moved to Mountain View Cemetery. Many local organizations were alarmed. More bones were unearthed in 1959 when additional school structures were added. They immediately took action and had those existing remains exhumed and placed in containers that now rest in a solitary grave on the property near the student parking lot.

In May 1963, a bronze memorial plaque was dedicated to the unknown buried pioneers on the school grounds. It features an open Bible made of marble and is encased in stone. It was dedicated by the Daughters of Mohave Pioneers Group. The plaque reads:

> *We humbly dedicate this ground the site of Kingman's first cemetery in memory of the founding pioneers who were interred in these hallowed grounds 1861–1920, erected May 20, 1963.*

The school remained Mohave County Union High School for some fifty years before later being renamed as Kingman High School. In 1973, the old three-story high school burned down. A new school was built (with more bones found) on Grandview, which housed a high school for another thirty years. In 1993, a new high school was built outside the Kingman city limits. The new Kingman High School North campus was opened for sophomores, juniors and seniors. Freshmen attended the older school (Mohave High School), which was renamed Kingman High School South. This became White Cliffs Middle School in 2006 and is where the memorial plaque and old cemetery grounds were located. In 2010, the old middle school was converted back to a high school.

Construction on the *new* Lee Williams High School (same location) began in 2010 and was completed in 2012. During the building of the new high school, strange things began to happen all over again. Workmen digging a trench near the bleachers discovered more human bones and suspected coffin rubble. Fifteen to twenty bones and bone fragments were found in a four-foot stretch of the trench near the football field, where games have been played for decades. They also found items such as jewelry and a brass nameplate. Excavation suddenly came to a standstill. The construction workers felt uneasy digging in an old graveyard. The idea of handling remains made them very uncomfortable. While archaeologists dealt with the remains, the contractor went so far as to contact a local tribe for a blessing of the land. The tribal elder performed a blessing ceremony to appease the spirits and reassured the workmen that they would not be followed home.

Over the years, there have been reports of hauntings at the school due to the theory that the "displaced souls" were unhappy with their final resting spots being disrupted and paved over with asphalt. Some say that ghosts began appearing at school events and the surrounding area, often wearing pioneer clothing or western wear.

Others noted they have felt unexplained cold spots throughout the high school building. The students and teachers note that there are certain areas in the building where they feel uneasy or try to avoid. One such spot is an odd, narrow passageway with a small, half-size door. They say it leads into a dark, windowless chamber much resembling a vault or a tomb. It is not used and nobody seems to know what the chamber was used for, but the tiny room was included in the building plans.

The school staff has noted several spirits that insist on remaining after school. They have heard footsteps in the hallways or behind them presenting that eerie sensation of being followed or that they are not alone. They have heard knocking on walls and doors and seen lights flicker on and off—enough to make any brave soul a little cautious. There are faint voices, children's laughter and an occasional disembodied voice demanding that they "go home!"

Some of the staff have even reported seeing a little girl who appears and urges them to play a game of ball with her. Students and staff insist that they have seen a man in a bowler hat and long black coat who seems to loiter around the area of the school building.

Perhaps the saddest tale of misplaced sprits concerns Jennie Bauters and Clement C. Leigh. In about 1903, Jennie Bauters—Jerome's most famous and loved madam—left Jerome and headed for a new boomtown called Acme (now known as Gold Road). Jennie's gambling suitor, Clement C. Leigh, followed her there, and they began living together once again. After a time, Jennie began to feel that he was becoming somewhat of a threat; at the same time, Leigh was certain that she was about to discard him from her lifestyle. In September 1905, Leigh needed money to settle a bad debt. Filled with anger and a gun in his hand, he bounded over to Jennie's place and demanded that she hand over all her cash. An argument ensued, and Jennie tried to flee the building. He chased after her, firing several shots at the frightened woman. One bullet struck and wounded her as she ran frantically out into the street. He approached the paralyzed woman, noted that she was still alive and fired a fatal shot to her head. He then pointed the gun to his chest and fired again. He lay down beside Jennie, placing his hat over his face to shield from the sun, ready to die. Instead, Leigh survived his suicide attempt and was carted off to the old county jail in Kingman. Jennie was mourned by all who loved her and laid to rest at the Pioneer Cemetery in Kingman. In 1907, justice was served when Leigh was hanged on the scaffold behind the jail. He, too, was buried at the Kingman Pioneer Cemetery.

As fate would have it, Jennie Bauters and her murderer are now buried in the same mass grave and entombed forever in the end zone of a football field. Part of Lee Williams High School sits over the grounds of the old cemetery, which lies under a portion of the football field and a set of bleachers. So, if you are ever attending a big football game at the old stadium and the excitement begins to magnify, beware that the rising spirits might be more than just the cheering crowd.

Lee Williams High School
400 Grandview Avenue
Kingman, AZ 86401

EL TROVATORE MOTEL

The El Trovatore Motel is one of the few pre–World War II Kingman motels still standing along Route 66. This historic Route 66 motel started as a service station in 1937, with a tourist court added in 1939, when you could get a room for just three dollars per night. The motel has a Hollywood theme and is located on El Trovatore Hill, a stony bluff that offers spectacular views of the Hualapai Mountain and Slaughterhouse Canyon landscapes.

Urban legend states that a pioneer family lived in a small settlement back in what was called Slaughterhouse or Luana Canyon. The husband worked in the nearby mines and at times would be away from the homestead for weeks at a time, earning money to keep his family clothed and fed. As in many tragic Old West tales, one day the husband left to work in the gold mines but never returned. Was he robbed and murdered? Did he fall ill? It is not known. Meanwhile, his devoted wife and children were left alone in the canyon with no means of support. The children were starving and wept for food. After some time, the mother went insane from the desperate sobs and wails of her starving children.

The voices of the children echoed throughout the canyon, and as the well-being of the family began to wither into the wind, their voices were often heard in the nighttime breeze. Soon their screams of starvation circulated all around the canyon. After many days, the mother could not bear to hear her children's painful screams anymore. Legend says that she murdered them and then took her own life.

Those who have dared to visit Slaughterhouse Canyon have testified to feeling the anguish that still fills the air. And on evenings when the air is very still and thick, it's reported that you can hear the screams of the innocent children and the anguish of the mother as she made the tragic decision to end their suffering.

Locals say that it was popular in high school to load a car with students and park in the canyon down by the remains of an old slaughterhouse shack. They rolled down the windows and waited quietly for "Luana." Invariably, there were some weird or eerie noises, which prompted the teens to get out of there—once was usually enough! Other ghost hunters report driving down the road that leads into the canyon and witnessing a mysterious woman wearing a black dress and dark veil as she walks down the side of the road. When they turn around to drive back, she is gone.

The fabulous road trip teams of Cemetery Crawl 9 were up early one Sunday morning and heading off to breakfast with the teams. Some of them

El Trovatore Motel
on Route 66. *Author's
collection.*

met up at Mr. D'z Route 66 Diner in the presence of a not-so-nourished
Elvis mannequin. Coffee talk at the table was about an unusual awakening
at about 3:00 a.m. in the morning when a good number of the crawlers
heard "children laughing and frolicking" in the El Trovatore Motel parking
lot. We later learned that hearing children in the parking lot of the motel has
been an ongoing phenomenon for many years. These ghostly children are
never seen but often heard by staff and visitors; they have become a large
part of local lore.

El Trovatore Motel
1440 East Andy Devine Avenue
Kingman, AZ 86401

CHAPTER 21
OATMAN

OATMAN HOTEL

The town of Oatman was chosen to honor Olive Oatman, a young Illinois girl who was captured and enslaved by a Yavapai tribal group during her pioneer family's journey westward in 1851. She was later traded to the Mohave tribe, who adopted her as a daughter and tattooed her face in the custom of the tribe. She was released in 1856 at Fort Yuma.

In 1863, prospector Johnny Moss discovered gold in the Black Mountains and staked several claims. He named one the Moss, after himself, and another after Olive Oatman, whose legendary story was well known in the area. For the next half century, mining had its highs and lows in the remote district until new technology reduced production and transportation costs. Oatman was served by a narrow-gauge rail line between 1902 and 1905 that ran seventeen miles to the Colorado River near Needles, California. New gold discoveries brought prosperity to Oatman in the early twentieth century. The opening of the Tom Reed mine, followed by the discovery of a rich ore body in the nearby United Eastern Mining Company's property in 1915, was celebrated as one of the desert's last gold rushes. The prosperous years of 1915–17 gave Oatman all the characteristics of similar gold rush boomtowns. At one time, the mines of Oatman were among the richest producers in the West.

The fire of 1921 burned down several of Oatman's smaller wood-frame buildings but spared the now famous Oatman Hotel. Originally called the

Oatman, Arizona street scene. *Courtesy of Route 66 Postcards.*

Durlin Hotel, the popular establishment was built in 1902 by John Durlin. It still reigns as the oldest two-story adobe structure in Mohave County. The historical landmark proudly boasts of being the honeymoon stop of actor Clark Gable and his bride, Carole Lombard, after they were married in Kingman, Arizona, on March 18, 1939. The Gable-Lombard honeymoon suite is one of the hotel's major attractions. The hotel has housed many miners, movie stars, politicians and travelers. Oatman has been used as the location site for several movies, such as *How the West Was Won*, *Foxfire* and *Edge of Eternity*.

The town's main employer, United Eastern Mines, permanently shut down its operations after producing $13.6 million worth of gold. The district had produced $40 million in gold by 1941, when the rest of the town's gold mining operations was ordered shut down by the government as part of the country's war effort, as other metals were needed. Fortunately, Oatman was located on busy Route 66 and catered to travelers driving between Kingman and Needles, California. This new lifeline was short-lived, as the town was completely bypassed in 1953, and a new, faster route was constructed between Kingman and Needles. By the 1960s, Oatman had been all but abandoned.

Although the hotel no longer accepts overnight reservations, you can still explore the former hotel rooms on the second floor. The historic building is

The Oatman Hotel was originally built in 1902. *Author's collection.*

now home to a museum that talks about the history of Oatman and some of the famous hotel guests who have enjoyed its accommodations during its heyday. Visitors and employees both agree that the building is quite haunted.

One legendary spirit is a miner who is affectionately known as "Oatie" by present-day staff members. The friendly poltergeist tends to perform small pranks around the hotel and its restaurant. Oatie is believed to be the spirit of William Ray Flour, an Irishman who frequented the hotel and saloons in its heyday. He was saving money so he could send for his wife and children to join him in Oatman. His family never arrived from Ireland, and this led him to more drinking in local saloons. Legend says that he died behind the hotel after a night of heavy drinking up in his room. The playful ghost has been seen raising the money off the bar and suspending glasses into the air and dropping them to the ground. Oatie likes to interfere with the music on the jukebox and hide things from the employees of the hotel. The spirit frequents room 15, and the imprint of his body has appeared across the bed.

Of course, the ghosts of Gable and Lombard are said to haunt the establishment as well. They continue to celebrate their nuptials and refuse to leave their honeymoon suite. Guests and staff have often heard the pair of lovers whispering and laughing from the room when it is vacant. One professional photographer stated that he took a picture of the empty room and was shocked when a ghostly figure of a man who resembled Clark Gable appeared on the print. Other ghost hunters have snapped photos in the room that captured unexplained oddities.

Paranormal investigators Debe Branning and Fallon Franzen chatted with Oatman Hotel employee Lynne as she operated a walk-up snack and drink window at the front of the hotel. The owners were getting ready to travel out of state for August, and they regularly close the museum, bar, restaurant during the hot summer month.

"Have you had any experiences with the ghosts?" we asked the young hostess.

"All the time," she smiled. "Why just the other day I was sitting here all alone in the building and I could hear someone going up and down the stairs. I turned around expecting someone to be standing behind me—and there was nobody there!"

"That would be eerie," Fallon nodded.

"And just about that same time I could hear what sounded like a tray of bar glasses crashing to the floor. I peeked into the bar, and everything was in its place. But things like that happen all the time here. The bartenders say a prankster ghost moves things around all the time! Some guests have noted seeing a man sit at the edge of the bar who vanishes before their eyes. It doesn't scare me. I always remember to greet them in the morning…and say goodbye when it's time to go home."

The gift shop manager reported that she spent one evening waxing and buffing up the floor. She was the only person in the building and was getting ready to close for the day. She turned around and found dusty footprints on her clean floor. Items are often moved about the gift shop, especially the small ceramic coyotes.

Colleen Sulzer joined us just as Lynne was reminded of another story. "I had one lady visitor tell me a spirit of a woman dressed in white sits on the staircase behind me and watches what I do all day."

"Have you seen her?" Colleen asked.

"No, but there are times when I feel like someone is sitting back there staring at me. I did see a lady all dressed in white standing on the balconies of one of the other buildings," Lynne said, smiling. "She had on white mourning veil over her face, and she was looking down. Maybe she is the same ghost and visits both of the buildings. A lot of the shop owners in town have claimed they've seen the lady in white."

A local named Angie recalled the time she encountered a residual stagecoach clambering down Main Street of Oatman. It was early in the morning, when the town is quiet and motionless. She suddenly felt a cold breeze and heard the sound of galloping horse hooves and the rolling steel wheels of the stagecoach rush past her. It sounded like there were small children laughing and giggling inside their ghostly chariot.

She also mentioned seeing a translucent gray figure of an old miner wearing what looked like a straw hat. He was kicking a tin can down Main Street as he made his way out of town. Could it been Oatie, heading up to the hills to work on his claim?

Oatman Hotel
181 Main Street
Oatman, AZ 86433

OATMAN'S "PEARL"

One of the popular attractions of Oatman is the array of burros that roam freely through the town, seeking snacks that the tourists can purchase for a small fee to feed them. The friendly livestock is not corralled at the end of the day. They simply retreat to the nearby hills to graze until it is time to entertain the Route 66 travelers the following day.

The townsfolk of Oatman like to share the ghostly tale of "Pearl the Burro." Legend states that there once was an old prospector by the name of "Howdy" who was rarely seen without his trusty white pack mule, Pearl. Together, they were quite the team, and they trusted each other as partners in the mines for many years.

The shopkeepers would smile every time the duo came into Oatman to collect supplies and gather food. Howdy didn't always have cash in his saddlebag, so he'd often settle his tab by trading a small bag of gold dust for their essentials. Folks say they were last seen together heading on the north trails out of town, back up to the mines. It was a late, dark, stormy evening in late October 1917.

Sadly, a few days later, Pearl was discovered in Oatman alone. She ran frantically up and down Main Street braying loudly in a panic. Her white hair seemed to glisten under the bold light of the full moon. Several of the townsfolk came out of the shops and saloons to try and calm the sorrowful burro down. They tried to catch her, but the frightened burro kept running away. Pearl turned around, stared at them with pleading eyes and brayed as if to urge, "Follow me! Follow me!"

No one understood her despair, so Pearl sadly disappeared into the dark night, alone. The old prospector Howdy was never seen again. Time passed, and suddenly Pearl began to appear on the streets of Oatman whenever there was a full moon lurking behind the dark, menacing clouds. She meandered down the street, braying mournfully for of the citizens of Oatman—still trying to get them to follow and rescue her partner.

Old-timers in Oatman still report that Pearl returns to town whenever there is a full moon. They encourage visitors to snap a photo of her, if they dare, and post on a bulletin board in town. But then again, if you see a white burro on the side of the road sadly braying in the night, you might want to try to ignore what you see. Don't follow the white burro into the hills—it just might be "Pearl the Ghost Burro."

CHAPTER 22
TOPOCK

OLD TRAILS ARCH BRIDGE

Topock is known for being a boating town, as well as being home to the Old Trails Arch Bridge (built in 1914), which used to be the Old Route 66 bridge and was featured in the film *The Grapes of Wrath*. The crossings of the Colorado River at Topock, including the Old Trails Arch Bridge, are also featured prominently in the opening credits of the movie *Easy Rider*.

Topock was originally called Mellen, a railroad station and steamboat landing, at the site where the Atlantic & Pacific Railroad built the Red Rock Railroad Bridge across the Colorado River in May 1890, after three earlier bridges were washed away by the river upstream near Needles. Planks were laid on the rails, and travelers paid a toll to cross the bridge in between trains. The town was named for Captain "Jack" Mellon, a forty-year Colorado River veteran steamboat captain and an owner of the Colorado Steam Navigation Company. The name of the town was misspelled as "Mellen" from 1903 to 1909 while it had its own post office.

The Colorado River Valley has been inhabited for more than ten thousand years as the home of the Mojave people, whose name is a reformed version of *aha* (water) and *macave* (along or beside). The word *Topock* (*toh* pahk) is also found in San Bernardino County, California, and derives from the Mojave word *tuupak*, itself derived from the verb *tapak* (to drive piles). Another translation says that it comes from *ahatopok*, which means bridge, for the railroad bridge built there in 1890.

Old Trails Arch Bridge over the Colorado River near Topock. *Author's collection.*

The National Old Trails Highway's route was laid from California to Kansas, and the road crossed the Colorado River at Topock. It was first assembled by using a ferry, but by 1916, the historic Trails Arch Bridge was constructed. Route 66 was aligned along the National Old Trails Road in 1926 using the same bridge, and during the 1930s, many farmers escaping the devastating Dust Bowl crossed it heading west seeking jobs in California. Old-timers say that when the migrant workers reached this area and first laid eyes on the Colorado River, they became euphoric. Some wept with happiness. This evoked emotions in the caravans of travelers much like the early seafaring immigrants experienced as they took in the view of the Statue of Liberty for the first time. But for some travelers, the road ended there. Many travelers faced armed police officers who turned them away as "undesirables" or as "Okies" and "Arkies," as they were profiled. Some were feared to be a health threat or troublemakers with the law. Often officers met migrants at the state line and told them to leave because there was no work or took the money they had for food. About 40 percent of these migrants who made it across the border picked cotton and grapes in California, earning one dollar per day. With emotions riding so high, does their spirited energy remain near the river?

In 1952, Route 66 was realigned, bypassing Sitgreaves Pass and Oatman. The new route ran along level ground close to the railroad—Kingman through Yucca. I-40 crossed the river in 1966 and replaced Route 66 altogether in the area.

One thing is for sure: whether it be good times or bad, the travelers along historic Route 66 will agree that the highway had become a symbol of faith and hope for the future.

The Old Trails Bridge is located several hundred feet south of I-40, where it crosses the Colorado River at Topock. To park and view the historic bridge, take the exit for Park Moabi—the first CA exit as you head west. Signs direct visitors to the park. Follow the Park Moabi Entrance Road north to its intersection with the National Trails Highway/Park Moabi Road. The first vantage point is from an old brick bridge nearly a mile from the intersection. You can park on the side of the road and walk down the old bridge top. The second vantage point is about two miles from the intersection. Drive along the National Trails Highway/Park Moabi Road past the first vantage point and intersection with I-40, then look for a historic concrete billboard and adjacent pullout area. This location provides the best scenic view of the bridge.

A toast to standing on the corner in Winslow. *Author's collection.*

PARANORMAL RESOURCES

TEAMS AND TOURS

Arizona Desert Ghost Hunters. www.adghosthunters.com.
AZ Ghost Adventures. www.azghostadventures.com.
AZ Paranormal. info@AZParanormal.com.
Crossing Over Paranormal. www.thecopscrew.com.
Friends of the Other Side. www.friendsoftheotherside.com.
MVD Ghostchasers. www.mvdghostchasers.com.
Phoenix Arizona Paranormal Society. www.phoenix-arizona-paranormal-society.com.
Phoenix Ghost Tours. https://phxtours.com/ghos t-tour.
Phoenix Haunted History Tours. marshallshore@gmail.com.
Southern Arizona Scientific Paranormal Investigators. www.SASPI.org.

BIBLIOGRAPHY

Arizona Champion. "Miss Mabel Milligan a Beloved Local Teacher Died Suddenly Thursday." November 9, 1923.

———. "More Rustlers Killed." September, 10, 1887.

———. "Terrible Santa Fe Wreck at Winona Yesterday." December 17, 1909.

Arizona Daily Sun. "Bribery Case Goes to Jury Late Today." August 13, 1947.

———. "The Ghosts of Ash Fork Hill." April 12, 2014.

———. "Williams Man Found Dead Near Seligman." January 3, 1956.

Arizona Republic. "Indian Miller…Charged with Death of Canyon Lodge Postmaster." June 22, 1926.

———. "Invitation to Hanging Episodes Are Recalled." April 13, 1936.

———. "Mystery Cave Cursed by Evil Spirits." December 3, 1967.

———. "Shooting at Holbrook." January 22, 1896.

———. "Youngster Killed by Accidental Shot at Truxton Canyon." September 15, 1924.

Barger, Matthew. *Holbrook Arizona Historical Self-Guided Tour Guide Book*. N.p.: Navajo County Historical Society, n.d.

Branning, Debe. *Dining with the Dead*. Phoenix, AZ: American Traveler Press, 2017.

———. *Grand Canyon Ghost Stories*. Helena, MT: Riverbend Publishing, 2012.

———. *The Graveyard Shift*. Phoenix, AZ: American Traveler Press, 2012.

———. *Sleeping with Ghosts*. Phoenix, AZ: Golden West Publishers, 2004.

Chief Yellowhorse Trading Post. www.yellowhorseltd.com.

Coconino Sun. "Gosh! Simplicio's Ghost Is Back." June 4, 1920.
———. "Three Mexicans Arrested Charged with Drain Murder." March 19, 1915.
Evening Herald. "Veteran Arizona Indian Trader Assassinated in His Trading Post at Allantown Last Night." June 28, 1915.
Find A Grave. "James D Houck, an Aged Pioneer, Ends Life with Poison." findagrave.com.
Flagstaff Historic Downtown. Walking guide. www.discoverflagstaff.com.
Gumeny, Eirik. "Ella's Frontier Trading Post." Atlas Obscura. https://www.atlasobscura.com.
Haunted Hiker. "Ghostly Tales from the National Parks: Petrified Forest National Park." October 29, 2012.
Hawkins, D. "Human Remains Discovery Haunts Kingman School Sewer Project." *Las Vegas Review*, July 30, 2010.
Hotel Monte Vista. www.hotelmontevista.com.
La Posada Hotel. Walking tour guide. www.laposada.org.
Legends of America. "Allentown, Arizona—Railroad Route 66 Town." May 2019. www.legendsofamerica.com.
———. "The Curse of the Petrified Forest." February 2019. www.legendsofamerica.com.
———. "History & Haunting of the Navajo Country, Arizona Courthouse." December 2020. www.legendsofamerica.com.
———. "Houck, Arizona—Home of Fort Courage." May 2019. www.legendsofamerica.com.
———. "James D Houck—Arizona Pioneer & Lawman." February 2020. www.legendsofamerica.com.
———. "Meteor City & Meteor Crater." February 2020. www.legendsofamerica.com.
———. "Oatman Highway." May 2019. www.legendsofamerica.com.
Lowell Observatory. www.lowell.edu.
Mangum, Richard, and Sherry Mangum. *Route 66 Across Arizona*. Flagstaff, AZ: Hexagon Press, 2001.
McClanahan, Jerry. *EZ66 Guide for Travelers*. N.p.: National Historic Route 66 Federation, 2019.
Mohave County Miner. "Another Gold Road Killing." September 9, 1905.
———. "Dr. Ford Accidently Killed." October 19, 1912.
———. "Sudden Death of W.D. McCright." March 13, 1915.
———. "Superstition of the Wallapai." June 28, 1919.

Mohave Museum of History and Arts. Kingman Historic Downtown walking map. www.mohavemuseum.org.

Mural Mice Universal. "Story of a Ghost Mural." www.muralmice.com.

National Park Service. "Old Trail Bridge." www.nps.gov.

———. "Querino Canyon Bridge." www.nps.gov.

———. "Walnut Canyon Bridge." www.nps.gov.

Nogales International. "Trading Post Man Attacked by Pet Lion." August 1, 1931.

Orpheum Theatre. www.orpheumflagstaff.com.

Rioradan Mansion State Historic Park. www.azstatepark.com/riordan-mansion.

Roadside America. "Giganticus Headicus." www.roadsideamerica.com.

Robson, Ellen, and Dianne Halicki. *Haunted Highway: The Spirits of Route 66.* Phoenix, AZ: Golden West Publishers, 1999.

Ross, Jim, and Shellee Graham. *Secret Route 66: A Guide to the Weird, Wonderful, and Obscure.* St. Louis, MO: Reedy Press, 2017.

Rowland, Jackie. "Oatman: History Recipes Ghost Stories." *Route 66 Magazine* (2006).

Sherman, Gene. "The Justice of the Peace Has God-Fearing Outlook." *Miami Herald*, July 6, 1967.

Snyder, Tom. *Route 66 Traveler's Guide and Roadside Companion.* New York: St. Martin's Press, 1995.

Sonderman, Joe. *Route 66 in Arizona.* Images of America series. Charleston, SC: Arcadia Publishing, 2010.

Williams News. "Harvey Hudspeth Killed by No. 9." May 6, 1921.

———. "Jos. McDaniel Killed." April 17, 1947.

———. "Torres Paroled Convict Murdered Victor H. Melick." June 6, 1919.

———. "Williams New Harvey House." June 15, 1907.

———. "Woman Brutally Murdered in Local Tourist Camp." May 7, 1926.

Winslow Mail. "Famous Guide Is Badly Bitten by a Gila Monster." July 3, 1925.

———. "Leorena Shipley of Winslow Drowned When Flood Caves Bridge at Cottonwood Wash." September 17, 1926.

Winslow.Town. "Earl's Route 66 Motor Court." May 17, 2019. www.winslow.town.

ABOUT THE AUTHOR

Debe Branning has been the director of the MVD Ghostchasers—a Mesa/Bisbee, Arizona–based paranormal team—since 1994. The team conducts investigations of haunted historical locations throughout Arizona and has offered paranormal workshop/investigations since 2002. Debe has been a guest lecturer and speaker at several Arizona universities and community colleges, science fiction and paranormal conferences, historical societies and libraries.

Her television appearances include an episode of "Streets of Fear" for FearNet.com (2009); an episode of Travel Channel's *Ghost Stories* about haunted Jerome, Arizona (2010); and an episode of *Ghost Adventures*, "Old Gila County Jail and Courthouse" (2018). As a paranormal journalist, she has investigated haunted locations including castles, jails, ships, inns and cemeteries, and she has taken walking ghost tours in the United States, England, Scotland, Ireland and Mexico. She has been the guest of the Historic Hotels of the Rockies and U.S. tourism departments in Carlsbad, Salem and Biloxi.

Debe is the author of *Sleeping with Ghosts: A Ghost Hunter's Guide to Arizona's Haunted Hotels and Inns* (2004), *Grand Canyon Ghost Stories* (2012), *The Graveyard Shift: Arizona's Historic and Haunted Cemeteries* (2012), *Dining with the Dead: Arizona's Historic and Haunted Restaurants and Cafés* (2017), *Haunted Phoenix* (2019) and *Ghosts of Houston's Market Square Park* (2020), as well as a series of three children's books, *The Adventures of Chickolet Pigolet: The Bribe of Frankenbeans, Murmur on the Oink Express* and *You Ought to Be in Pig-tures*.

Visit us at
www.historypress.com